Point to Point

The meanderings and musings of my life

MARY GIDLEY

Dedicated to my sister Marilyn

she marched to a different drummer

✦

FOREWORD
By: Hannah McDonald

I remember when I was 21, just graduating film school, and my grandma mentioned that a Swedish filmmaker wanted to do a documentary on this thing she did in the 70's. "What you'd do Grandma?" "Oh, I was a part of this psychological experiment where ten strangers and I floated across the Atlantic Ocean on a raft."

"...*You did WHAT?!*"

Meet my grandma, the author of this book, Mary Gidley. She said it as casually as if she was telling me what she had for breakfast. "How have you not told me about this before?!" She just shrugged. Because to her an adventurous out-of-this-world life is simply the norm, and she wouldn't even think to boast about her countless awe-inspiring experiences. This is where I come in.

I ended up tagging along to Sweden for three weeks to help on the documentary about the raft experiment. It was on that trip that I first really got to know my grandma—not as just my playful tennis instructor, storyteller, and donut supplier, but as the sharp, fearless, and off-beat person she is.

I know I'm biased but I feel that objectively my grandma has lived a pretty amazing life—never buying into a consumeristic ego-driven lifestyle to gain money and status but rather choosing to measure her life in experiences. She's never lived to impress anyone else; she's lived to love her life.

The memoir you are about to read will take you through time. From the raucous adventures she and the neighborhood kids had in the vacant lots of 1940's Wisconsin, to the rugged Sausalito fishermen lifestyle she eagerly dove into in the 60's, all the way to modern times as she struggles to maintain her sanity in this technology obsessed world. Her pin-sharp memory and candid wit will keep you laughing and pang your heartstrings as you reminisce with her through the ups and downs of a life well lived.

As her motivation manager, editor, and technological guide in writing this memoir, we have built a connection that I deeply cherish. My grandma has become a true confidant, mentor, and friend to me.

I also have a new understanding that so much of who I am comes from who she is. My adventurous spirit, that in recent years has been my most defining quality, totally mirrors hers. (Although, my grandma at 25 on the cover of this book, sailing a boat to Mexico while raising her first child makes my current mid-twenties "adventures" pale in comparison).

She has been and will always be a huge inspiration to me, so I am thrilled that those not quite lucky enough to share her DNA now have a chance to share in the awe of hearing her story. But don't take my word for it. Without further adieu I present *Point to Point: The Musings and Memoirs of my Life* by Mary Gidley.

Enjoy the ride.

TABLE OF CONTENTS

ACKNOWLEDGMENTS

I'm not sure if writing a memoir was my idea or my granddaughter Hannah's. All I know for sure is that it never would have happened without her.

She served as my reader, editor, formatter, designer, and tech person. Her cheerful, optimistic attitude brought joy to the project. When my fingers were too clumsy to type on a laptop, she typed my stories in over the phone. She never complained.

We got together first in a coffee shop in Santa Ana. On other occasions she flew to Marin and stayed with me in my apartment. In the mornings when I woke up Hannah would often be cuddled up by the electric fireplace in the corner of the couch working on the book. The coffee would already be bubbling.

During the recent years we have shared many other adventures. She's come to Sweden and to Mexico with me. We play tennis and do yoga together. A few years ago, Hannah made a wooden frame for a photo of us sailing. It reads, "Adventure is worthwhile in itself." This book has been one of those adventures.

The best compliment I ever got was when Hannah said she thought she was becoming like me. I'm not sure what she meant, but God help her.

Thank you Hannah, for everything.

PART 1: EARLY LIFE

ALMOST BURNING UP

I remember the time when I almost burned up, even though I was a baby. We lived on Lakeside Street in Madison, Wisconsin. I was a fat little baby, so fat that the rolls on my legs made me look bow-legged when they tried to stand me up. If I had burned up, I would have resembled a fat charred Bratwurst.

I was sick with bronchitis, with a bad cough, and congestion in my lungs. I was put to sleep in my crib upstairs in mother and daddy's room. The hired girl at the time was Elvira. She laid me down in the crib and plugged the steam vaporizer in next to me. It was supposed to have water in it to add moisture to the air and clear up my nose and lungs. She put a pink blanket over the top of the crib to keep the warm steam in. Then she plugged in the vaporizer and walked away.

The flames woke me up. It was so hot. I cried and cried. It was my father downstairs who first heard me crying, and as I was not a crying baby, he sensed something was wrong. He ran upstairs. When he came into the room the pink blanket was in flames and I was trapped in the crib. My father's arms reached in and snatched me up through the fire. He carried me downstairs. I was all right. I was alive. His arms smelled of singed hair.

Later I wasn't sure whether I made this story up or if it actually happened, and I never really asked. The verification came fifty years later at my sister Marilyn's funeral in 1991 when Elvira, then a thin, shaky old woman, came up to me and apologized for plugging in the vaporizer without putting any water in it.

We may all have had a close call like that as an infant or a small child. I know my own children did.

One of the worse times was in Mexico. My husband Cass sent Lupe and Sharon, who were 4 and 7, out in the little Sabot to sail by themselves. He was standing on the shore watching. I came out of the house holding baby Memo in my arms. Suddenly we realized that they didn't have their life preservers on! The wind was kicking up and the little boat, captained by Sharon, started heeling over as they tacked back and forth. We were too far away for them to hear us calling. I will never forget how helpless I felt and how crazy with fear. Any moment it looked as if they would capsize.

Fortunately, Cass saw some boys paddling around nearby in one of our war canoes. He yelled at them to come over and climbed into the canoe. He and the boys paddled furiously out to where Sharon and Lupe were floundering in the little sailboat and escorted them home. Ironically, this was the only time the girls didn't have their life preservers on. Cass was always insistent that they wore them. He had seen too many fishermen's kids drown. I was extremely relieved and thankful to whatever gods there were that day.

THE VAKE

"Meet you in the vake!" was our cry. It was three vacant lots right next to each other. I loved the vake. The vake was full of wonders and tradition. I couldn't wait to throw off my school clothes and pull on a pair of old jeans, a shirt, and tennis shoes and run out the side door. Because we lived near a lake, the vake had a whitish soil. We could find tiny snail bodies, but nothing much else would grow there. We played every game and every sport in the vake. We even pretended to cross-country ski on cheap skis with straps.

In the middle of the vake was a huge deciduous tree, not easy to climb because the trunk was wide in girth and the limbs were far off the ground. I got stuck in the tree once and I couldn't get down. A mother came out of a house and brought me a ladder. It was the tree where we had our basketball hoop. No backboard, nothing fancy, just a fire-place poker that had been heated and bent into a round shape and nailed to the tree by someone's father.

Our meeting place in the vake was the apple tree with its gnarled sturdy branches that dipped close to the ground. It was simple to climb, the branches easy to step on, and different crooks in the limbs were seats for us. It became our airplane. We pulled and tugged on branches to steer the imaginary craft and parachuted out of the tree when our mothers yelled at us to come home. This was during and shortly after World War II. We sang "Coming in on a Wing and a Prayer" as we parachuted to safety.

The apple tree hid us from our enemies, especially the mean and nasty newspaper boy and his sister. We blended in with the leaves, far enough away from the sidewalk to be out of danger from the rocks they would throw at us. The hard little green apples we would throw back never hit their mark.

Sometimes I was the first one at the vake. Perched above the ground in the apple tree, watching for some other kid to come out of the neighboring houses, I was happy to just sit and wait. I liked the view, looking out over the neighboring houses and the lake.

One of the parents gave us an old picnic table which was set down near the tree. It became our laboratory, our art studio, and our stage. We did experiments, making concoctions out of anything anyone could bring from their houses. We mixed all kinds of ingredients—toothpaste, shaved crayons, smashed snail shells, wild strawberries, and the hard, bitter, wormy green apples from the tree. Then we would entice our younger siblings to drink our concoctions out of Dixie cups. They didn't tell on us because, according to the code of the vake, "telling" was a most serious crime. We did not want any adult meddling in our affairs.

We played softball in the vake, with a tree for first base, a fire pit for second, and the sidewalk by the street for third. Home plate was a worn spot in the dirt. Although we had a regulation ball, the gloves were old and flimsy. If you didn't have a glove you played with your bare hands. We played tackle football, hoping not to get tackled by a big kid named Brock, who we thought weighed about 200 pounds.

The main gang of the vake consisted of me, my older sister Marilyn, Patsy Gibson, Cleo Kuhnau, Jackie and Joanne Straus (when they were allowed to play by their overly protective mother), Bobby and Jimmy Mueller, and Betty Scott, whose father made our basketball hoop. Brock and some other kids came now and then.

Patsy Gibson was a champion athlete. She won the National Speed Skating title as a teenager. During the summer she would come to our door and ask for me. I would go running with her. It was her way to train when there was no ice on the lakes.

Patsy had a nice mellow father who walked around the lake to go to work at the University of Wisconsin, but a terrible mother. Mrs. Gibson blew a shrill whistle when she wanted Patsy to come home.

One day climbing a tree, Patsy caught her pants on a branch and ripped them. She was afraid to go home because she would be beaten.

All of our mothers were scary, although in different ways. Cleo's mother would call her into the kitchen and tell Cleo how unhappy she made her. She would tell Cleo to turn the gas on and open the oven door so she could stick her head in. Then there was my own overworked housewife mother who spanked us with a yardstick and called us "lazy good for nothings."

But we had the vake and we also had the lake. In the summer we lived in the water, playing tag under the raft that our fathers had anchored out for us. We jumped in and dove from a tree that hung over the lake. My father's boat was tied up next to the pier. There were crayfish, carp, perch, minnows, blue gills, and weeds in the water. When the water got warm and greenish with algae, the weeds would grow into a tangled mass. They weighed down your arms when you tried to swim the crawl. Sometimes we swam across the lake, feeling as though we had swum the English Channel. I also liked washing my hair in the lake, ducking under the water to rinse it clean.

In the winter the lake froze over. Standing on the surface you could hear a boom as it froze down deeper. The cracks showed how thick the ice was at the time. When it snowed we shoveled the snow off the ice to make a rink and played hockey. Sometimes we played with no skates, just in our rubber boots. The rule became "no raising the puck" after I got a goose-egg on my forehead from a puck that came flying over the ice.

Outside in the vake and lake we were free, away from rigid rules or adult supervision. We never had helmets, shin guards, knee pads, etc. There was only one time I remember being stopped. Patsy and I were digging a tunnel in the vake. We were making a secret passage to a future underground dwelling. Mrs. Straus saw what we were doing and stopped us. She said it could cave in on us and bury us alive. After that we had to be content with building igloos and houses above ground.

Grandpa Lee, Marilyn, and me

GRANDPA'S FARM

We drove "down home" to grandpa's farm almost every weekend. The farm was about 30 miles south of Madison, over some rolling county roads with dips that made your stomach flip-flop. My father drove fast just to thrill us and hear us squeal. When the snow was very deep we had to leave the car at the top of the road. My grandfather would be waiting for us with a team of horses and a sleigh to take us the rest of the way. If we had our sleds in the trunk of the car he would tie them to the back of the sleigh. Then we were pulled through the snow, laughing and trying to hang on.

Grandma and Grandpa did not have electricity, indoor plumbing, or running water. The "new-fangled" telephone was a fixture on the wall with a long black beak-like speaker and a crank. When you picked up the receiver the operator would ask who you were calling. The line was shared so all conversations were overheard by whoever wanted to listen.

A rain barrel sat on the front porch and the water in it was used for drinking, cooking, and washing. The wood stove in the kitchen was a huge black cast iron affair. Flames darted about trying to escape. A dipper in a large pail of water sat on the kitchen sink. Everyone drank from the same dipper. Water from the rain barrel was heated for baths that took place in a washtub on Saturday nights.

A sinful side to these strict Norwegians was their love of sweets. If you take a look at the Lee family cookbook, it's heavy on desserts. Salads feature jello and grated carrots, or green jello with pineapple chunks and marshmallows. One Sunday when my two cousins were also at Grandpa's farm we had a contest to see who could eat the most pancakes. I ate twenty something, but my cousin Dick ate thirty-six.

There was also my grandfather's famous "sugar bread." My grandmother made all the bread from scratch. When it came out of the oven, my grandfather would saw off thick slices of the warm white bread, spread on a coat of home-churned butter, and then shake a thick layer of white sugar on it. We loved it. We put butter on almost everything (and I still do).

I remember Grandpa bouncing my sister on his knee and saying "Feela filla, feela filla, feela Phyllis." I think it meant something endearing in Norwegian, the language he always spoke when he talked to Grandma and ordered her around.

At night a kerosene lamp was carried upstairs where we slept. It made yellow patterns of light on the ceilings and floors. There were grates in the floor of the bedroom and if we wanted to know what the adults were doing downstairs, we hunched over the grates straining to hear and to see what was going on. There was a chamber pot in the bedroom if you had to pee and big high beds covered with homemade quilts that were piled on when we went to bed, for there was no heat. Our noses were as cold as a dogs' when we woke up in the morning. We stayed under the covers waiting for the smell of bacon from downstairs and for the big stove in the parlor to be fired up.

The two-story farmhouse had an attic that held trunks full of treasures like the hats, dresses, veils, shoes, and memorabilia from my mother and Aunt Ruth's school days. We played dress-up, tripping around in their shoes, and wearing red velvet jackets and hats with veils.

Sometime between Thanksgiving and Christmas, when we were down on the farm, my mother and grandmother would pull out the Montgomery Ward and Sears catalogues and have us kids look through them so Grandma could order our Christmas presents—a new game, a pair of pjs, a stocking cap, maybe a sweater or a blouse. My mother would measure us with a tape-measure to get the size right. We looked forward to looking through the catalogues knowing that Christmas was coming. The old catalogues were recycled by using them as toilet paper in the outhouse. I remember a movie my dad filmed of shy five-year-old Fuffa coming out of the outhouse in her pajamas.

I was thirteen when my grandfather died. The farm was sold and all of the animals, machinery, and tractors were auctioned off. We kids never went there again. Grandma, who had dementia, came to live with us half of each year. The other half of the year she was delivered to my Aunt Ruth and Uncle Ted and their two boys who lived in Nebraska and later on in Denver, Colorado.

Grandma was a challenge. She used to pick our things up and move them to strange places. We would ask her, "Where are my boots?" or, "Grandma, what did you do with my scarf?"

She would look at us quizzically, shake her head and shuffle away. Sometimes we would find our boots, books, or clothing in the garbage. Sometimes we would never find them. One day I found grandma eating my dog's food.

Grandma lived many years being shuttled back and forth, but finally became too much for my mother and my aunt to take care of. She eventually died in a nursing home in 1959. One time in high school I wrote a poem about her. The assignment was to write in iambic pentameter. This is the way it went:

> First you fell and broke your hip
> and then you lost your mind.
> We packed you up and shipped you out
> with others of your kind.

...and through the snow to grandfather's house we go

Grandpa and Grandma

Our house on Lakeside Street (1937-1950)

MY MOTHER

My mother had a huge influence on how I dealt with emotions. When I was about three years old she bought me a live turtle from the dime store. Tubby came in a shallow glass bowl that had a rock with a fake umbrella on it. Tubby was my first pet and I cherished him. Every afternoon after my nap I would rush out to the back steps and observe him as he swam in the shallow water or climbed up on the rock.

One afternoon he wasn't in the bowl. I became frantic, crying and sobbing and searching the steps and the driveway. This was terrible. I cried and cried. My mother came outside in her apron to see what was the matter, I ran to her crying "Tubby's gone"! "For heaven sake," she said, "He was just a dime store turtle." But I couldn't stop sobbing. "Quit your crying or I'll give you something to cry about," she said and went back in the house.

I stayed outside looking for Tubby until dark. I even searched the tall grass of the vacant lot next door. I was only three years old but I was not the same inside. I vowed never to go to her with my feelings again. She taught me that feelings were not good, and I was a quick learner.

There were some good times too. I have happy memories of my mother reading books to us at night when we were little and listening to us pray, "Now I lay me down to sleep…" Then she would tuck us in and I guess she kissed us good-night before we went to sleep, but I don't remember any kisses or hugs from her.

Christmases were more good times. We were never disappointed. After dinner consisting of lefse, lutefisk, and oyster stew, we were hustled upstairs and gotten into our pajamas. Then we settled down next to Mother as she read to us. It was hard to concentrate on what she was reading because we knew that very soon Santa would be coming to our house in person. We got Santa twice, once at the beginning of his long journey and once more in the middle of the night after we were asleep. That's when he filled our stockings and ate the cookies we left out for him.

Upstairs our ears perked up listening for the sound of bells. Downstairs the lights would be dimmed. We strained our ears to hear what was going on, and then came the "ho ho ho's" and the ringing of bells and we were called downstairs.

We tripped over each other a little fearfully as we descended the staircase. The only lights on were the lights from the tree and the two Santa bulbs on both sides of the mantel piece, (which I still have). Santa had poor eyesight and it was worse in the dim light. My father helped Santa hand out our presents, whispering to him who each one was for. Then Santa would announce the name and one of us would step forward.

"Have you been a good little girl this year?" he'd ask. I always said "yes," hoping he wouldn't know about the little white lies or of my unmerciful teasing of my little sister Phyllis, which often provoked her into charging me with fists flying.

✧

Shopping was something my mother did also, but I'm not sure she enjoyed it. She always wanted me, or one of us, to go with her. The payoff was a chocolate ice cream soda in a tall glass with a long straw at Walgreens or Rennebohm's drug stores. I didn't pay much attention to what she was buying, she would pick it out and hold it up to make a decision. I just wanted her to hurry and be done so I could get my ice cream soda. If she asked me, I'd say, "Yes, you should buy it."

At the end of the shopping we sat at the counter on stools and ordered. I twirled around happily. When I drank my soda, I took my time, capturing the delicate whip cream and sipping slowly through the straw. I would use the long-handled spoon to slowly fish out the ice cream. "Hurry up!" she would say. I think my mother hated shopping too—that's why she dragged me along.

One time when we were just finishing at the drug store my mother discovered a small coin purse under the counter. She picked it up and put it in her purse. I was shocked because I was still the idealistic little girl who believed in being 100% honest, and I thought my mother was also totally honest.

There was another time that she shocked me. We were driving home through the Bush, where mostly poor Italians lived, when a little dog ran out in the street. My mother hit it and kept going. I looked back and saw that the dog was lying in the street and some people were gathering around. "You hit the dog," I said. She didn't look at me. "It was just a little bump," she said. We drove the rest of the way home in silence.

A couple of years ago I heard about the *Church of Stop Shopping*. Oh, how that appeals to me! I've always absolutely hated shopping. I hate going into stores looking at the piles and piles of stuff, now mostly from China. Mind boggling, dizzying, disorienting—I feel like I want to throw up when I see those container ships coming under the Golden Gate Bridge. Recently one had 15,000 containers on it—full of stuff like plastic toys, dolls, underwear, capri pants, jeans, sweaters, socks, tech toys, and appliances for people to buy buy buy so more will be produced and thrown away because the other is out of style, out of fashion, slightly broken. My slogan for several years has been "make do," and if something breaks, "Oh well, I can get along without it."

I'm trying to remember other good things about my mother. She was taller than most, and pretty when she wasn't frowning. She was the prettiest of all my friend's mothers, and I was happy about that. Unfortunately, I look more like my father.

Daddy was shorter than most men and acne had scarred his face, but he was a charmer and a jokester and people loved him. He was eleven years older than my mother and already had a balding head and a paunch, although he was a skinny man. His name was Athanasius but everybody called him Nace. One time as a joke, he dressed up and went trick or treating to the house next door. "And what's your name little boy?" my friend's mother asked. "Nacey Gartland," he said in a squeaky little voice, holding out his bag. He never got tired of re-telling that story.

My father smoked cigarettes. The downstairs little bathroom was filled with smoke after breakfast, and the rest of the house stunk of smoke too. All of us complained, but nobody knew that smoking was killing him. The health consequences were not known or publicized at that time. He died of a heart attack at age fifty-nine. Both Marilyn and I started smoking in our late teens. I finally kicked the habit in my late thirties when I realized that trying to run or play tennis while continuing to smoke was not going to work.

When I was about sixty years old, my daughter Lupe gave me a "Grandma Remembers" book. I was expected to complete it for my grandson Riley. When I was in Wisconsin I tried to squeeze some personal information from my mother. I had her sit down in the living room. "So, Mother, how and when did you and Daddy meet?" She gave me a scathing look. "What do you want to know that for?" Then she got up and walked away.

As I said before, I looked more like my father than my mother. But as I get older, I notice that I am beginning to look like my mother did in her old age. (Also, sometimes when I look in the mirror, I see a resemblance to Uncle Lawrence!) To sum it up, my relationship with my mother was difficult. She died at ninety-four. But one time a therapist said, "No, your real problem is with your father." I will try to explain that later.

Daddy holding Marilyn, my mother, and Grandpa holding me

THE WAR YEARS

I was four years old and lying on the daybed in the parlor at Grandpa's farm on Sunday, December 7, 1941, when the announcement came over the radio that the Japanese had bombed Pearl Harbor. Everyone was shocked into silence. The solemn talk afterwards was about the war we were now getting into.

The war meant some changes for everyone. Two of the men who worked for my father painting barns were drafted. As a result, my father had to post bail to get men out of jail to work for him.

Many goods were rationed. One needed a certain number of stamps to buy meat, gas, tires, oil, butter, or nylon stockings. Billboards along the road reminded people that we all needed to be part of the war effort. One of the signs read "Is this trip necessary?" and had Uncle Sam in his tall hat wagging his finger sternly at you.

One fall day when it was starting to get cold my father went down to check on the furnace, which was a coal burning monster in the basement. Low and behold, inside the furnace in the ashes he discovered a package wrapped in butcher paper. Inside was a large

14

roast. My parents were astounded. Where did it come from? How did it get there? The only explanation was that Rosalie, our maid at the time, had hid it there planning to take it home to her family. She denied it. We ate it.

Margarine was substituted for butter, but in Wisconsin, the dairy state, you could not buy margarine that was colored like in the rest of the country. It came as a white block and then you squeezed a packet of color into it to make it yellow. Everyone was also encouraged to have a victory garden. We dug up a small plot in the backyard and grew carrots, lettuce, and radishes in rows marked by seed packets. When we worked in the garden pulling weeds, we were swarmed by mosquitos. It was not fun for us kids.

One day in kindergarten the elastic in my underpants broke. It wouldn't have been so bad if I was wearing pants, but little girls only wore dresses. And it wouldn't have mattered so much if we hadn't had to get up and skip around in a circle to the music. I was in danger of having my underpants slip off my hips, fall down to my ankles, and onto the floor. I didn't want to tell the teacher so I skipped along with my elbows dug into my sides to hold the underpants up. Fortunately, it was wintertime and I could pull on snowpants when school was over.

In the newsreels in the movie theater the Japanese were slanty-eyed, yellow-skinned, ugly little men. We were taught to hate the Japs and the Germans. One of our neighbors were the Strauses. "You're German aren't you?" I said to my friend's mother. "No, we are Americans!" she said. I knew I had said something wrong.

When I was seven years old in 1944 we celebrated VE Day (Victory in Europe) and then VJ Day (Victory against Japan). The war was over. We decorated our bikes with crepe paper and paraded around the block waving little American flags and tooting the horns that our parents had brought home from a previous New Year's Eve party.

Shoveling snow is fun!

GRADE SCHOOL IN MADISON

I started kindergarten at Franklin School, about three and a half blocks from our house on Lakeside Street. The school was built of brick, just like the third little pig's house. About eight years ago, the last time I was in Madison, the building was still there and functioning as a school. The playground was full of tan bark and plastic structures instead of our metal monkey bars and swings, but otherwise it looked the same.

All my grade school teachers were older unmarried women, except for one youngish art teacher who had a nervous breakdown, and Mr. Ralph our sixth grade teacher who frequently fell asleep in class. In kindergarten we just played. We started the half-day singing "Oh What a Beautiful Morning" with the teacher playing the piano. The rest of the time we listened to stories, ate some snacks, and played some more.

Nobody ever drove us to school. When the wind was blowing snow in our faces, we walked wrapped up like mummies. In sleet, rain, and hail, we walked. When the wind chill or temperature dropped below zero, we walked. Bucking a head wind was a challenge, but not as bad as the threat that the older boys posed who ambushed us, throwing snowballs and ice balls at us little kids.

It was a complicated strategy planning your walking route home. If we thought they were waiting on Lakeside Street, we took the back way home by taking South Shore Drive, and vice-versa if we thought they were waiting to attack us on South Shore Drive. Ice balls were the most feared. Snowballs made the night before when the snow was slushy were left overnight to freeze solid by the next day. The hard ice balls would be lined up at the curb like ammunition.

When you finally made it home from school you couldn't forget to take your boots off before you came into the house. When you were covered with snow you had to go down into the basement and your mother or a sister would whack you with a broom to get the snow off before you took your jacket off and were allowed to come upstairs.

The hub of our South Side neighborhood were the businesses by the school. On one corner was a drug store, and kitty-corner was Mrs. Sheely's little grocery and candy store. A bell tinkled when you came in the door alerting Mrs. Sheely, who lived in the back. One time my friend Patsy stole some candy before Mrs. Sheely could get to the front.

Across the street from the school was Bernie's Market where we bought our groceries. You went up to the counter and gave him a list. Then Bernie or a clerk went and gathered all the items for you. This was not a problem because there were no non-fat, low-fat, low sugar or gluten free products. Just the originals. Crackers were either graham crackers or saltines, not flax-seed chia almond thins with no extra salt and added garlic flavor.

A lot of the food came in cans, later some came frozen. There was not much fresh produce in Wisconsin with its short growing season, I don't remember ever reading a label that said a product came from Chile, Mexico, France, Germany, or China.

A few days ago I opened some frozen peas from the package that I frequently buy from Trader Joe's. Turning the package over I saw that the peas were from Germany! What? I do not understand why they don't sell the peas that are grown in California. I grew some in my son Memo's garden, so why are they being transported from Germany?

Anyway, next to Bernie's Market was Fanny Farmer's Candy Kitchen, where they made a variety of chocolates, but they didn't sell them retail. Next to the Candy Kitchen was the Hardware store, where nothing came in plastic or in elaborate shrink-wrapped packaging. You could buy a single nail, screw, or battery there.

When I graduated from the eighth grade, our yearbook was a flimsy little mimeographed pamphlet of very few pages. My friend, Sally, and I were co-winners of the scholarship award. All the kids, about twenty of us, were of various shapes and sizes. I was the tall and awkward looking girl with broad shoulders who was holding my little pin.

Sally and I were born just a few days apart in the same hospital. She always still calls me on my birthday and catches me up on the news of our classmates, both dead and alive

After Franklin School then on to the big time, Central High School. It was located in downtown Madison. We took the bus, or walked around the lake, or over the railroad tracks. During the winter we walked across the frozen lake to get to school. We didn't have to worry about getting hit with ice balls anymore. Everyone thankfully had outgrown that stage.

Marilyn, Me, Mother, and Fuff

DADDY'S LITTLE GIRL

I was a round-faced, fat-cheeked little kid in a snowsuit with a helmet type hat on my head. I sat on my tricycle by the sidewalk, unable to ride it. A woman came walking by. "What a cute little boy," she said, and smiled at me. I heard what she said and I was happy for the mistaken identity because somehow I already suspected, even before I could reach the pedals, that men and boys had the most fun in life.

I had already seen my mother angrily picking up after us, cleaning, and cooking while my father just sat in his chair reading. She yelled at us and threw our books across the room, but she didn't say anything to my father as he read his detective novels. My mother vacuumed around him, merely asking him to pick up his feet.

Sometimes daddy supervised us mowing the lawn or raking the leaves, but in a lazy easy-going way, and he never did any work inside the house. Later on I heard that he and our next door neighbor Ole would have a drink or two in Ole's basement. I don't think either my mother or Ole's wife knew this, or maybe they just chose to look the other way.

My father's business was seasonal. He really only worked six months of the year. He was an ex-school teacher and principal who during the depression went into a barn painting business with one of his brothers. They also owned a farm together. My father managed the barn painting; my Uncle John ran the farm and raised registered Black Angus cattle. All the cows had pedigrees and were sold as calves to 4H kids or for breeders.

My father named a lot of the cows after my mother, hence there was "Belle's Delight", "Belle of the Ball", "Dreaming of Belle", etc. In late spring and early fall we had a cattle drive, driving the cows and the big old bull from the farm to the green pastures of Rocky Run several miles away. Every once in a while the big old bull would stop and turn around and look at us kids with our puny sticks. We were ready to run if he charged.

There was a marsh near my father and Uncle John's farm, and when the Canadian Geese were migrating and flying over they would shoot one or two down. Because it was illegal, they put newspapers over the windows in the basement while they cleaned the poor mangled goose. My father and his brothers also hunted pheasants and deer in season.

During the winter my father made some business trips, talking to farmers about their crops and getting them to commit to having their barns painted in the spring and the summer. Daddy liked to have me go with him as he drove around to get jobs. While my father went inside to talk to the farmers, I sat in the car, reading a Nancy Drew or Black Stallion book and waited. The payoff was apple pie a la mode at a little cafe in Rio, Wisconsin.

I did a similar thing later in my life. When my husband Cass was delivering fish in the rain and fog and cold, I sat in the cab of his truck knitting a little blue and gold baby sweater. Did I finish the baby sweater before my first baby Sharon was born? Definitely not. Knitting was not my thing. And there was no pie pay-off this time.

Madison was called the "City of Five Lakes," and fishing was my father's biggest passion. At first we lived on Lakeside Street and when I was fourteen years old we moved to the brick house on South Shore Drive. Then the lake, actually Lake Monona Bay, was right across the street. From there one could go by boat into Lake Monona proper, and from there through some locks to Lake Mendota, the biggest lake in the chain, and via other channels to

Lake Kegonsa and the other lakes.

In Monona Bay, my father fished for crappies and perch. There wasn't much else except the big lazy carp that were considered a crap fish and no good for eating. My father fished in the winter too. When the lake was frozen, he and I walked out on the ice, me towing a sled of gear. Then we drilled a hole in the ice. You had to keep scooping out the chunks of ice that kept forming over the hole. In those years there was no high-tech gear and no warming tent. You were just standing, staring at the hole, and beating the sides of your body with your arms trying to keep warm. I don't remember catching any fish.

We had a rowboat and a five horsepower motor. Our neighbor boy, Michael, had a canoe, and Ole, the adult neighbor, had a speedboat capable of pulling us on skis. One day he pulled me underneath the railroad trestle, making me swerve from side to side, dangerously close to the rocks. He was laughing his head off, trying to throw me off. My mother was furious with Ole when we came in. I was surprised. She didn't want me killed. She must love me, I thought.

My laid-back father

DR. VARKER AND MY TEETH

We liked our sugar bread but we paid for it. My teeth were never very good and I blamed my mother because she never drank milk, not even when she was pregnant. I never blamed the sugar bread. There was one check-up when I had eight cavities. Dr. Varker, our old white-haired dentist did not believe in Novocain, or else he didn't know about it. He was from the old school. He smoked cigarettes so his fingers were yellowed and his breath smelled like nicotine. His entire office and waiting room smelled of cigarette smoke.

At the base of the stairs to his office was a "No Soliciting" sign. I didn't know what crime that referred to as I dragged my feet up the stairs.

When it was summertime and hot and humid, there was no air-conditioning in his office. Nobody had AC in those days. The waiting room was dark, stuffy, and creepy. There were the normal lamps and magazines, but also a giant stuffed alligator who stood with one "arm" cradling an amber colored ashtray filled with cigarette butts. The ashtray was the size of a Frisbee. Most people, and all men, smoked. The alligator had a grinning mouth, full of sharply pointed teeth.

My older sister Marilyn usually went first. She was the brave one. Then it was my turn. Dr. Varker wore thick glasses making his eyes appear huge. "Let's see. Which one are you?" he asked. His memory, as well as his eyesight, was not that good. I tried to turn away to not smell his breath. Then he started drilling, and drilling, and more drilling. The window had blinds yellowed by smoke with slits of daylight coming through. I stared at them, all tensed up as I gripped the edge of the chair.

The drill went deeper and deeper into the tooth and the nerve. "Just a little bit more" he would say as he attacked again and again with a drill which was as noisy as a jackhammer and agonizingly slow. "Just a little bit more..." When I couldn't stand it anymore, I would grab his hand and try to pull it away. "Don't do that or we'll never finish," he said. We would both be sweating. He was shaky and worn out afterwards. For me it was torture. When it was over my mother made another appointment and the receptionist gave us all a big round sucker.

A goal in my life has been to keep my teeth and never have false teeth. For this reason, I am diligent about flossing and have an extensive tooth cleaning regime. It's something all of my family members are painfully aware of. Saving my teeth, however, has been a costly goal.

At this time in my life I have had three implants, about a dozen crowns, many fillings, and several extractions. The money I have spent helped put my dentist's two sons through medical school, but I'm still set on keeping my own teeth. I floss and brush religiously. A song I sang to my children and grandchildren goes like this: "When you wake up in the morning and it's quarter to two, and you don't know just what to do, you brush your teeth, cha cha, cha cha, cha cha cha cha..."

When I was seventy years old I saw a periodontist who said that I should be able to keep my teeth because I have very deep roots. I recently read in the newspaper that he had died suddenly. Maybe the secret to having your teeth your entire life is to die young.

MOTHER AND MORE HOME LIFE

My mother's purpose in life was keeping us five girls clean and well-fed and the house in order. A James Thurber cartoon shows a woman's large body encircling a house. She's scowling at a little man approaching the front door. That woman was my mother. She scowled at all of us. The house was her domain, which was one reason we always wanted to be outside. "Don't step on my clean floor," and "Don't splatter toothpaste on the mirror," and "Don't leave the hall light on," are examples of what she would say.

Mother was also the one to punish us if we didn't hear her call us in for supper. If we broke a plate, or a vase, or a lamp, or spilled something on the rug, we were in trouble. One night when she and my father had gone out, which they occasionally did, the baby-sitter, who was almost as young as we were, was chasing us around the house. We were running through the living room, into the dining room, through the kitchen and back into the living room when the floor lamp got knocked over and broke. We tried to put it back together, but it was wobbly and wounded, and we knew my mother would be angry. Marilyn and I got spanked and the babysitter wasn't called back.

Every time my mother got out the yardstick and whacked us (Marilyn and me) I always flinched and cried, usually before she even hit me, and I kept wailing how sorry I was. But not Marilyn. She took it silently and stoically, which angered my mother even more. Then one day the yardstick broke when she was hitting Marilyn. She never used the yardstick on us again.

My mother's chores included cooking, cleaning, washing clothes, and ironing. In the early years there was not much grocery shopping because milk and groceries were delivered. Mother fed us canned green beans, (which I choke on now), other canned vegetables, and canned fruit. We never saw an avocado, or broccoli, or any other kind of lettuce, except iceberg lettuce.

Washing clothes did not mean you tossed your dirty clothes into an automatic washer and dryer, and pressed a button. Oh no. In the basement we had a wringer-type wash machine. There was no dryer. After washing a batch of clothes, my mother fished them out one at a time with a long stick and poked them into the wringer from which they came out all flattened like boards with the water all squished out and fell into one of two rinsing tubs, a warm water one, and a cold water one. After the final rinse, the clothes were put through the wringer once again. They then tumbled into a clothes basket.

When it was summer, my mother would carry the basket out-side and hang the clothes up one by one on a clothesline in the backyard. I have a memory of my mother with a mouthful of wooden clothespins hanging up clothes and all of us being frantically called to come out to pull the clothes down if it was starting to rain. If it was winter or stormy, my mother hung them in the basement. It could take several days for the assortment of underwear, socks, pants, shirts, blouses, skirts, sheets, towels, etc. for seven people to dry, and we would be ducking under the limp wet forms for days.

Washing was only one of the labor-intensive activities of my mother. She also ironed all of our clothes, including the underwear, the towels, and the pillow cases and sheets. The sheets were put through a machine called a mangle that was set up in my father and mother's bedroom.

My mother sewed dresses and pajamas for us, and she put on missing buttons, and darned our socks. She also sewed dance costumes every year for Marilyn, Phyllis, and me. We took lessons in both ballet and tap (not our idea). Over the years Marilyn and I were ladies in-waiting, musical notes, college girls, snowflakes, and waterfalls. One day the instructor lost her patience and called us "elephants." It didn't bother us, we called her "ashcan butt Irma."

The three ballerinas—Marilyn, Phyllis, and Me

There is a framed 8x10 photo on my dresser in my bedroom of us three older girls wearing dresses my mother made. Mine is checkered and has a scalloped neckline. Marilyn and Phyllis's dresses are checkered pinafores, with shoulder straps and white blouses attached underneath. Cass stole the picture from my mother's dresser when we visited one time. I didn't have the courage to return it, even after Cass and I were divorced.

Later in life, my mother kept on sewing, doing needlepoint and crocheting, and making little dresses for her six granddaughters. I never liked to sew or cook or clean. I didn't want to be like her, and I could never do anything right anyway, according to her. One time I wanted to iron my own gym uniform. After I started to iron it, she snatched it away saying that I was doing it all wrong, and she finished it herself. I stormed out of the room vowing to never try to do anything like that again.

The only time my mother seemed relaxed was after she had some beer during the neighborhood poker parties. Smoke filled the little nook in our kitchen. There was laughter. Seeing my mother smiling and laughing was very odd. When my grandmother was staying with us, my mother would hide her can of beer.

My mother made one attempt to break out of her housewifely chains. When Marilyn, Phyllis, and I were older, and our little sisters Patty and Mickey did not need as much care, my mother got a job in the Candy Counter at Sears. Every afternoon she put on white shoes and a white uniform with a little green apron and went out the door to work. None of us liked the change.

"What's for supper?" my father asked. "Who's going to cook?"

One day my mother pulled out a frozen packaged dinner of macaroni and cheese in a wax-covered cardboard box. "You just have to heat it up," she said. When suppertime came my father put the macaroni and cheese in the oven, (but left it in the box). He told one of us set the table and went back in the living room to read.

Marilyn and I got some canned peas out of the cupboard, found a can opener, and plopped the peas into a pan. Patty and Mickey were hungry. I said, "Shut up, so are we." The timer on top of the oven went off. I poured the milk, and we sat down to eat. There was an unpleasant smell of burning wax coming from the oven.

My father came in and took the melted and deformed box of macaroni and cheese out of the oven. Marilyn asked if maybe he should have taken it out of the box before he put it in the oven. He gave her a blank look.

It tasted terrible. We had to hold our noses when we chewed the mac and cheese and none of us could swallow it. My father said, "There's nothing wrong with it." (Of course, my father smoked two packs of Lucky Strikes every day and his taste buds as well as his heart and lungs were already destroyed). After supper we cleaned up with no mother to give us any orders or directions.

To have a job, to get out of the house, was huge for my mother. She was always nervous about being late and bustled about doing her hair, putting on her uniform, and gathering her purse, as we sat sullenly watching. She wore a name tag with "Belle" on it. She really had a name besides "Mother?"

When she came home at night she would have candy samples or outdated chocolates for us. She was animated and talked about the other women who worked at the candy counter. She had friends and she socialized with them. Her face was brighter. The frozen frown was gone. She seemed almost happy.

Mother worked at the candy counter for a year or maybe more. I'm not sure why she quit and became a housewife again. When my father died at age fifty-nine, she could have gone back to work. She was only forty-eight years old, but for some reason she chose to stay home with Patty and Mickey, who were both teenagers. When Mickey, the youngest, was ready to leave the nest, my mother cried and pleaded for Mickey to stay.

Several years later Marilyn and her husband moved back to Madison, and my mother became very involved in helping raise Marilyn's two kids. Mother also got herself a dog.

The Stolen Picture
I'm 8, Phyllis is 6, and Marilyn is 10

Some of the Lee family (I'm the baby)

ANCESTORS—A LITTLE HISTORY

I am a half-breed, (half Norwegian, half Irish). The two sides have been at war in me ever since I was born. (At least that's what I used to think.)

On the Norwegian side, my mother's side, my great-grand-father, Hendrik Lee (the last name changed from the Norwegian spelling of Lie) was born in 1838. He came on a boat when he was nineteen years old, and made his way to Luther Valley in southern Wisconsin. The rest of the family had already immigrated there, or maybe they joined him later. There are conflicting stories.

Luther Valley was one of the first and largest Norwegian settlements in America. One day looking on the internet, I saw how beautiful Norway's Hallingdal Valley was, and I wondered why on earth they left. Then I read that their families were too big to support on the amount of farmland available, which meant that if they didn't leave, they faced starvation.

Letters written back to friends and relatives enticed more people to leave Norway and come to this area in Wisconsin where everyone spoke their language and ate lutefisk and lefse on the holidays. In Luther Valley, the weather was about the same as it was in Hallingdal

Valley. There was land to be had and plenty of opportunities to work. By 1860 there were 44,000 Norwegians in southern Wisconsin.

Soon after arriving, my great-grandfather, Hendrik, and three of his brothers enlisted in the army to fight in the Civil War. It was an all Norwegian regiment, and as a result of signing up, they gained their citizenship. Hendrik fought in the battle of Vicksburg and sent a letter home mentioning the miserable conditions and how he had gotten a bullet through his hat. When they were on their way home, one of Hendrik's brothers got jostled off the over-crowded train. He was found by a farmer in Illinois, but died of his injuries a few days later.

My Norwegian great-grandmother, Barbara Norman, came from Trondheim, Norway, but I don't know when she came here or anything more about her, except that she married Hendrik and they had ten children, eight boys and two girls.

My grandfather, Leonard Gustave, the fifth boy, was born in 1875. He was a farmer, like most of them. He once told me the story of his grade school teacher mentioning a certain farm to be the best in the area and that whoever got it would be very fortunate. My grandfather then turned to proudly indicate the red barn with L.G. Lee in big block letters, the cornfield, the hog house—the coveted farm that he learned about as a boy, was all his.

What I remember is that my grandfather was a tall, lean, and sometimes stern man who had a limp. On one foot he wore a shiny black boot that was built up to compensate for a leg that was shriveled due to polio. As he got older, he used a cane. I learned that he wasn't just a farmer, but also a musician. He played the guitar and the piano. He and his band traveled to perform at various social functions. I now have his old pitch pipe. It's over 100 years old and still works. With it, I can tune my guitar without any blinking digital lights and without batteries to replace.

My grandmother was Bessie Lee, (nee Norman). She wore thick glasses, heavy brown stockings, and always deferred to my grandfather.

All of these Norwegian ancestors and relatives were hardworking people, big on family, and very religious. The Lutheran

Church was the focal point of the community. A Norwegian Bible cost my grandfather $12, (equivalent to about $340 today). To pay for it my grandpa and one of his brothers husked corn for the pastor.

Gustave Lee, my grandfather, died at age seventy-five in 1950. I was thirteen years old. According to my father, he died reciting the Lord's Prayer. The day he died, we kids were at home in Madison, not knowing what was going on "down home." We just knew that grandpa was sick. When my parents got home, my mother was too broken up to say anything and disappeared with her grief.

✧

On my father's side, my great-grandfather, Patrick Gartland, was born in 1815 in County Meath, Ireland. Of my great-grandmother, Anastasia Sinnott, I know nothing except her name. Patrick and Anastasia settled in Lowville Township about thirty-five miles north of Madison.

My Irish grandfather, John Gartland, was also born in County Meath, Ireland, but was brought to Wisconsin when he was a one-year-old. His first wife died and left him two children. John's second wife, my grandmother, was Mary Redmond. She was born in Wisconsin in 1856.

I never met either of these grandparents. Both died in 1936, one year before I was born. John died at age eighty-six, and Mary at age eighty. The amazing fact about my grandmother Mary is that she first married at the age of thirty-seven and gave birth to four sons in her forties. She was forty-eight when the baby of the family, my father, Athanasius (Nace) was born.

In a photo of the Gartland boys, my father is a baby in a long white gown, propped up on a very high chair. He's slightly hunched forward, like he can't sit up by himself yet. The three older boys, my uncles John, Bernard, and Lawrence, stand stiffly beside him. They are dressed up in suits and look like little old men.

When my Irish grandfather, John Gartland, died in 1936, it was written in the local newspaper that he was "one of Lowville's substantial farmers" and of my grandmother that she was one of Lowville's "most respected women."

Although most of my family on the Irish side were also farmers, they appeared much more relaxed and fun-loving than those on the Norwegian side. They were Irish Catholics, although my father was never a church-goer when we were growing up. They were also Democrats, in contrast to my Norwegian grandfather who was a die-hard Republican. My father loved needling my Republican grandfather on politics.

When my parents, Belle Lee and Nace Gartland, were married, I'm sure they did not have the blessing of either side of the family. They were married by a justice of the peace. To resolve the religious differences, neither of my parents belonged to a church and none of us were baptized when we were born. When I was young, not having a religion bothered me immensely.

Because my Irish grandparents had already died, we kids had much closer ties with the Norwegian side of the family. Every year the Lee family would gather for a reunion at a park in southern Wisconsin. After everyone had eaten their fill of the dishes that the women had prepared, and had dessert and coffee, the young children performed. They did a dance, sang a song, or recited a poem.

Another tradition of the reunion was to honor the oldest and the youngest member of the Lee family who were present. Grandpa Lee, was the oldest when he was in his seventies, the same year that my sister Mickey was the youngest. One year recently, my sister Mickey and I thought it would be a treat for my mother, who was in a rehab center, to go to the reunion. We rented a van to take her there. The plan backfired. Sliding around the back of the rented van in her wheelchair, she was not happy when we got there. She claimed the title of being the oldest, however, at age ninety-three. The Lee reunions seem to be a thing of the past, when now I would probably be the oldest.

✧

I recently fell more in love with the Norwegian side of my family, and a little less in love with my Irish side. After reading the seven volumes of the autobiographical novels of Karl Ove Knaus-gaard, I realized that Norwegians are not all uptight and religious, or sober, at least not anymore. In another book written by an Irish author I discovered that in those years the men were often sentimental sloppy drunks and the women led unhappy lives with no birth control, no independence, and no power.

My Family Tree

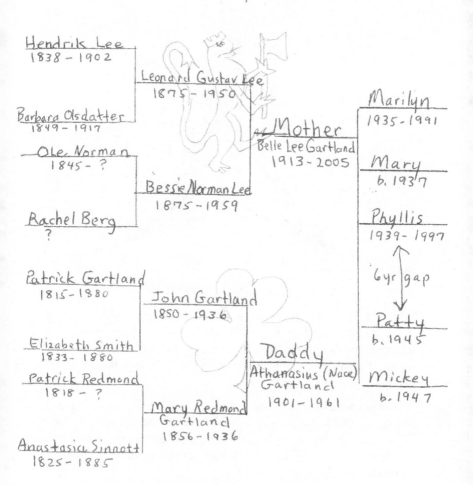

Hendrik Lee
1838 - 1902

Leonard Gustav Lee
1875 - 1950

Barbara Olsdatter
1849 - 1917

Ole Norman
1845 - ?

Bessie Norman Lee
1875 - 1959

Rachel Berg
?

Mother
Belle Lee Gartland
1913 - 2005

Marilyn
1935 - 1991

Mary
b. 1937

Phyllis
1939 - 1997

6yr gap

Patty
b. 1945

Patrick Gartland
1815 - 1880

John Gartland
1850 - 1936

Elizabeth Smith
1833 - 1880

Patrick Redmond
1818 - ?

Mary Redmond
Gartland
1856 - 1936

Daddy
Athanasius (Nace)
Gartland
1901 - 1961

Mickey
b. 1947

Anastasia Sinnott
1825 - 1885

33

MY GROWING UP PERIOD

In fifth and sixth grade some of the girls were already starting to develop breasts and to wear makeup, but not me. The boys were beginning to show an interest in them and it wasn't because of their brains. Physically I would not mature until the eighth and ninth grade, which was later than anyone else.

I was both looking forward to and dreading having my period. I went to a camp in northern Wisconsin one summer. One of the girls in my cabin called it "falling off the roof." My mother was non-communicative regarding any topic having to do with sex or menstruation. We were on our own.

It happened on a wintry night. I was fourteen years old. I had put on my heavy coat, a scarf, and boots and run outside to go to the neighbor's house. The snow was crunchy underfoot and the sky

34

sparkled with stars. I ran the block and a half to Betty Scott's house to watch their TV, the first in our neighborhood.

The television set was housed in a huge wooden cabinet, but the screen was tiny and the programs all in black and white. But just seeing anything on TV was amazing—even though most of the programs were of wrestling with two giant guys grabbing each other, rolling around, and grunting.

While I watched in their darkened living room I suddenly felt a wetness in my pants. Startled, I got up. Betty asked me if I was ok. "Yes, why?" I asked. "Because you're making a funny face," she said. I excused myself to go to the bathroom.

Yes, indeed. There were blood stains in my underpants and I knew I must be finally having my period. I felt like shouting the news. When I ran home under the stars and on the cold white crunchy snow I sang to myself of my new status. "I'm a woman now. I will have babies, lots of them…" Oh, a new world had opened up to me that night.

After my parents bought a TV one of my favorite programs was *The Waltons.* I wanted to have about a dozen kids like them. We would live in a large rambling farmhouse and all the kids would pitch in and work together with the mother and father. At the end of a program the Waltons wished each other a good night and the lights would go out in each room one by one. It was beautiful how they all loved and appreciated each other.

When I first got my period, I was ecstatic. Later the reality of wearing a sanitary belt and dealing with those bulky pads was not so great. The pads had to be changed often. Sometimes the menstrual blood spilled over the sides of the pad, staining and forming crusts on the edge of the underpants. We, (Marilyn and I), balled them up and put them in the laundry basket. My mother soaked the panties in bleach and washed them without a word or comment.

I regret to say that I am also guilty of not saying anything about sex or menstruation to my own children. It was a taboo subject, like death and dying. Being a human is to be an animal, but humans often deny this. We are not exempt from the laws of nature, but we like pretending that we are.

GOOD GIRL/ BAD GIRL

I was a good little girl up until about the age of ten. Then I realized that it was no longer cool to be the smart one in the class—the one who always raised her hand, who never talked out of turn, who concentrated, and listened, and who empathized with the teacher when the other kids acted up and caused trouble. I sat there in my little desk never complaining or even squirming, (although now I can't sit still worth shit).

I was good as gold—too good! This first came to light in the third grade. We had a tiny old gray-haired teacher named Miss Duncan who always picked me to take the milk money to the office. One time a boy named Charlie Willadson objected. "Why do you always pick her!" he demanded. I don't remember what she answered, but right then and there the two of them came to blows. Charlie was at least as tall and a lot bigger than frail Miss Duncan. Her glasses were knocked off in the tussle and Charlie ended up with a long scratch on his arm. All of us kids were shocked, and I felt even worse because they were fighting on account of me.

Did I then take the milk money and deliver it to the office? Probably, because I always did what I was told. One time when I was obeying a rule, it almost killed my mother.

It was a winter day. I came into the house, took my heavy jacket off, and sat down on the steps to take my snowy boots off. I heard my mother's voice from upstairs, but I couldn't get my boots to come off. There was a strict rule that you had to take your boots off before you came in the house. Marilyn came home a few minutes later and recognized the urgency of my mother's call for help. She thumped upstairs in her snowy boots and jacket, while I continued to wrestle with my boots.

I kept whacking the heel of my boot against the side of the stair. Some minutes later my sister and mother came downstairs. My mother's face was white. She was wringing her hands and stroking her arms. "Didn't you hear me, Mary?" she said, her voice unusually shaky and weak. "Why didn't you come when I called?" I figured this was a silly question. Later on my parents had my hearing tested, even though it was obvious to me why I hadn't responded to my mother's call for help.

What had happened was that my mother was vacuuming upstairs and took hold of the metal pipe under the sink. Then she grabbed the plug of the vacuum cleaner that was in the outlet. Electricity started to flow through her and she couldn't let go. She was getting weaker and weaker, and her voice was getting softer and softer. My sister saved the day. If she had sat down to take her boots off, my mother would have been dead. When Marilyn got upstairs, my mother could barely whisper, "Unplug the vacuum."

When I was a little girl, I believed in being strictly honest. One time we were taking the train from Madison to Omaha to visit my aunt and uncle and two cousins. My father and mother went up to the window at the train station to buy the tickets. Marilyn was sitting down reading her book, but Phyllis and I went up to the window with my parents. Children under five were free. When the ticket seller asked how old Phyllis was, I proudly blurted out, "Phyllis is five." My parents looked at me with disapproval. So much for honesty. They got away with buying only two children's tickets anyway because the woman did not realize that Marilyn, the girl sitting behind us reading, was part of the family. The "Phyllis is five" story was retold many times, and it always made me feel stupid and ashamed.

When I was young I had an unreasonable fear of authority, whether it was of teachers, policeman, doctors, nurses, nuns, or priests. Any person in uniform or in a position of authority could make me quiver in fear. This continued even into adulthood. It was a conditioned response that was hard to break.

Yes, I was a good little girl, but there was one bad thing that I did early on in life. When I was in kindergarten, a little boy got hit above the eye with a large block. It was thrown by me, good little Mary Gartland. Oh-oh, I saw blood running down his face and he started crying. Then the school nurse came and took him away. He was going to the hospital. He would need stitches.

The teacher sat us down on the rug in a circle. "Now boys and girls I want to know who threw that block." She scoured all the faces, mostly those of the boys who are the rowdy ones. "Did you throw the block that hit Jimmy?" No one said anything. I froze. "Boys and girls, we will sit here all the rest of our time, maybe longer, if nobody says who did it." More silence. I was never under suspicion. Some of the girls were, but not me. Not good, well-mannered Mary.

Why did I throw the block? Maybe just to see how far I could throw it. I already had a good throwing arm. The next day Jimmy came back to the kindergarten room with a huge bandage on his forehead. I never confessed.

✧

When I was in second grade we had a new principal, one who was obsessed with spelling. He introduced himself by popping into our class with a surprise spelling test. The next day he came in with the results. I had only missed one word, everyone else did not do as well. I was a marked girl.

Every year the school sent one student to the City Spelling Bee, and then, hopefully, to the State Finals. I was the runner-up when I was in the sixth grade. Another girl who was in in eighth grade won overall. The principal made us come sit in his office every morning before school and spell the words that he dictated.

The following year I didn't want to win. I missed words intentionally. At first he couldn't believe it. There was the word "etiquette." He kept insisting that I could spell it correctly, but I figured out many ways to misspell it. He finally gave up.

By the seventh and eighth grades, good girl Mary Gartland was pretty much history. One day my friend and I were sent to the office because we defied the rules and wore jeans to school. At that time girls were required to wear skirts or dresses. We got a lecture for our rebellion and were sent home to change.

My bad girl look

CORN DETASSELING

You had to be at least 5'4" tall to get hired and dumb enough to want to do it. They didn't seem to care how old you were. I was 5' 4" by the time I was in seventh grade, but I didn't sign up until I was in the eighth grade.

We assembled in front of Bowman's Dairy on Park Street and they picked us up at the first light of dawn. We were city kids dressed as field hands in long sleeved shirts and jeans, heavy shoes, wearing straw hats, bandanas around our necks, and carrying man-sized lunch buckets that banged against our knees. Every one of us swaggered with our new found importance as wage earners.

They loaded us into the back of open bed trucks that wobbled and swayed as we headed for the fields. Even though I had been born there, once we left town, I never knew where we were. We took back roads and country roads that I had never been on before. The landscape was one vast sea of barns and cornfields.

Our big boss was Blaney Seed Farm, producer of hybrid seed corn, an important enterprise in the economy of southern Wisconsin. Their signs dotted the roadsides and the highways along with Burma Shave signs.

Our job was to walk through the green arms of waving and beckoning corn, and decapitate them. We were to pull the yellow tassels off the top of every stalk in our row so they wouldn't pollinate the next row. We were told that if we missed one seductively waving tassel the entire field would be ruined. They lined us up on the edge of the cornfield and sent us down the rows in formation. Unplanned fertilization was as taboo as an unwed mother.

In the early morning, the edges of the wet leaves sliced across my arms and slapped me across my face. Later in the day, the sun made me drip with sweat like I was a cube of melting butter. I slapped at millions of mosquitoes that fed on my arms and my ankles. I was a strong girl but what was demanded of us in the cornfield required will power as well as brute strength. My arms ached and I stumbled often.

After working for five hours, we opened our lunch buckets alongside the truck on the edge of the field, hunting for a piece of shade and a place away from the mosquitos and bugs. We ate flaccid bologna sandwiches, cookies, and fruit hunched over in the dirt, then back to work.

I was a conscientious worker. When a tassel was stubborn I didn't just break it off, or ignore it and walk on, (as some did). I'd brace myself in the slippery mud and pull and pull until it let go. I was a surgeon at work performing a difficult operation.

All the other workers would already be out of the jungle of corn, drinking slugs of water. I couldn't believe it. Because I was almost always the last one out of the field I was singled out for some harsh words by our crew foreman.

The foreman was one of my classmates—a big, loud, red-faced girl who at school was always trying to set me up to fight. I hated her and feared her. She might as well have had a huge whip in her hand. She would yell at me for being too slow and holding up the rest of the crew.

I would not get any rest because the minute I appeared she would send us back up the next rows. If you have ever been in a cornfield it is an unsettling experience. You do not know where you are until you pop out on the other end. We never thought about quitting. I didn't think that it was an option. My best friend and I griped and moaned.

On the way home one day, a sudden lurch of the truck threw us all together, a tangled pile of sweaty bodies. We looked at each other differently. My friend's face became flushed and her eyelids fluttered at the boy who ended up with his head in her lap. He had thick curly black hair, a square jaw, and a well-muscled body. When she said "goodbye" to Pat I knew she had a crush on him.

A flash of fear struck me. Something was happening. We were sprouting up like the corn and developing those damn tassels.

Our house at 723 South Shore Drive

HE LOVED ME, MICHAEL

Michael became our next-door neighbor when we moved to South Shore Drive. He was physically mature for his age, and a superior athlete. At the City Swim Meet, Michael blew the other boys his age out of the water. He swam the crawl with his head up, which makes it even harder. He was also talented in baseball, track, and football.

Michael was the strong and silent type, with a slightly sadistic streak. He and another neighbor boy rigged up an electric shocking machine in his garage. At first, they experimented on stray cats, but later they tried it on my little sister Mickey and her friend. Michael went to Catholic schools. His parents were Catholic, although we seldom saw his mother because she never came out of the house. We didn't know at the time that she stayed in because she was an alcoholic.

Michael and I played at being pioneers and/or Indians. One time, Michael and I went hunting and killed a squirrel with the gun my father had given me for my birthday. We skinned and cooked it in the vake, nibbling on the tiny pieces of flesh. We realized that one squirrel would never make a meal.

Michael and I went spear fishing from his canoe. I paddled along the shore in the muddy greenish-brown water, and Michael stood in the bow watching for carp. Every now and then he launched his spear, thrusting it into the body of a big fat lazy brown carp. He was the Pathfinder and I was his squaw.

When Michael was sixteen he acquired a jeep. He wanted me to take a ride in the jeep one afternoon. I assumed my sister was invited too. When we ran outside to join him he frowned and said, "I don't want her to come." I found this a little odd seeing that we were all part of the same gang. I climbed up in the jeep and waved goodbye to my sister.

We bounced along, and I hung on. He drove to a construction site at the outskirts of town and turned in, ignoring a "No Trespassing" sign. Then he got a little crazy and it got a little scary. Michael tore up and around the mounds of fresh dirt like a madman. I tried not to scream. We churned up the hills, the jeep tilting from one side to the other as we came careening down. We left deep tracks in the soft red dirt.

Michael had an evil grin on his face as he stomped on the gas. *Ok, what was this all about? Will I make it home alive?*

When we parked in the street next to his house, I thanked him for the ride and started to get out of the jeep. But he stopped me. "Don't go yet," he said. He took my hand and stroked my arm and stared out into the night. This was almost scarier than the ride.

Then it started to rain, the drops splattering down and plastering my hair to my head. Michael put up the top. We sat there longer in the rain with the top up. Finally, he said he liked me and could we go again the next night. "Yes, that was fun," I said, as if I loved charging up and down a construction site in the middle of the night.

I ran home, grabbing the wet slippery railing and making my way up the back steps to our house, wondering again what this was all about.

In the following weeks I became his girlfriend. Besides our activities together, sometimes we just hung out on my back steps. Other times Michael and I explored various spots in Madison. One was the UW arboretum, a beautiful preserve of trees, plants, and trails that was not far from where we lived.

Down one of the trails, natural springs bubbled out of the ground and trickled over the rocks. An abundance of bright green watercress flourished there due to all the water. I remember one warm day Michael and I walked down to the water's edge and sat down in the soggy grass. I had just washed my hair. Michael reached up slowly and with trembling fingers started to stroke my hair. He marveled at its silkiness. I didn't know how to deal with his adoration of me.

This went on all spring. Michael said he loved me, although our relationship never went farther than holding hands, hugging, or a quick kiss. Then he told me that he wanted to marry me. This was getting too serious, I thought. I hadn't told him that when school was out, I was signed up to be a camp counselor in New Jersey. I would need to break the news.

When I finally told Mike, he didn't like it. He took my face in his hands. "Don't go," he said. I told him I'd already signed a contract. He tried to talk me out of it. In the next few days he brought me little gifts. If I didn't marry him he said that he would become a priest.

The night before I left, Mike came over after dark and we sat on my back steps. He ran pieces of my hair through his fingers. He was crying. He put his arms around me and hugged me. The fireflies on that superhot humid night electrified the air.

I kissed him and said, "I'll be back. You can write to me." He patted my hand. I was somewhat relieved to be getting away from him and our strange relationship.

When I was at camp I got a letter from Michael every day, often two letters. When we got our mail my name was called again and again. The other counselors teased me about all the letters! It was embarrassing. When I opened the letters in my tent, they basically all said the same thing, that he missed me and would I write to him.

I finally wrote, saying that I didn't want to hurt him, but would he please stop writing so many letters. Abruptly all the letters ceased. When I got back from camp, Mike didn't come over to see me. He didn't come outside anymore, or at least I didn't see him. No more fishing for carp, no more jeep rides.

Over the years when I went back to Wisconsin, I watched for him. One time I think I saw him run to his car from his house. I wanted to say that I was sorry. His intensity had scared me and he was too young, especially to talk of marrying me. (Although I was flattered to be chosen).

A few years later in college, I wrote a story about Michael for a creative writing class. My instructor told me to send it to a magazine called *Seventeen*. An editor wrote back with favorable comments but wanted some changes.

I didn't do it. I wish I'd saved that story for my memoirs.

Did Michael become a priest? I vaguely remember finding out that he had become a fireman and was living in Waterloo, Wisconsin.

TO YELLOWSTONE WITH NOLA

I must have been sweet sixteen. I had a driver's license and my friend, Nola, had a '47 Pontiac. We hatched a plan to take a month long trip to Yellowstone Park and the Grand Tetons. We would sleep in the car, or on the ground in an old canvas tent that we would anchor by pounding wooden stakes into the ground.

My mother was not thrilled—two teenage girls taking off on their own, but she knew enough not to try to stop me. When I got my heart set on something, I wouldn't listen anyway. My father never tried to tell me what to do.

Nola was two years older than me. She wasn't a close friend, but she had a car. My idea of roughing it and going without luxuries— like a bed, a house, regular meals, a bathroom, or a shower, appealed to me. *Ah, to be on my own and away from those annoying little sisters, especially Mickey.*

We set out towards the end of summer. I was going to be a junior in high school and Nola had just graduated. We had very little money, but that didn't bother us. We had optimism, and we were excited about the adventure.

In three and a half weeks we checked out all that Yellowstone and the area had to offer—the gurgling mud holes, the faithful geysers, and the magnificent snow-capped mountains of the Grand Tetons.

We cooked our food over a campfire. It all tasted delicious, even the smoky and burnt bites. We took long hikes and met friendly campers. One night a bear nudged the side of our tent. "Is that you, Nola? Stop pushing on the side of the tent!" I turned on my flashlight and saw that Nola was sound asleep in her bag. I lay there petrified until dawn knowing that some large creature was outside roaming around. The next morning most of our bread and cheese had been eaten, presumably by a bear.

At the end of August, the nights were getting colder and the weather was changing. We needed to head home to Wisconsin. We were dirty, tired, and broke. We stopped at a store in a little town and bought a loaf of white bread to go with our two cans of pork and beans and the last of our brown sugar. We ate the beans cold right out of the can. For dessert we put brown sugar on the bread, which tasted surprisingly good. It reminded me of my grandfather's "sugar bread," (but without the butter or warm homemade bread).

When Nola and I were welcomed home, we were grubby and disheveled. Since we had not bathed for a week or more, taking a bath was suggested.

I drew the clean, warm water into the tub, and added some bubbles. I got in and the water changed color. I had the nicest, weird ethereal feeling of my body lifting up and floating above the water. When I looked down at my stomach, there was a hollow where my stomach used to be, and my ribs were showing. When I dried myself off, I was on a different planet, weighing a lot less than on Earth. I felt like an angel that was lifting off and going to Heaven. (I had lost about 10 pounds).

I liked the feeling so much that afterwards I began eating just tiny bites of food, and little by little more weight dropped from me. Soon I was on my way to being anorexic, although the label and diagnosis were unknown in those years.

They sent me to our family doctor, a mellow man who dismissed my weight loss as me having "some kind of bug," but he thought I would get over it. I had all of the classic symptoms of an anorexic. I would dream of food, although I would eat very little. I nibbled at my cold cereal in the mornings, never putting milk on it, only water. At dinner I had a bite or two and that was it.

At one point I was down to 98 pounds, and my period stopped. Then I was scared. This did not fit in with my plan of having a large family like "Cheaper by the Dozen" or "The Waltons." I also read that if you get too thin, you will start growing fur-like hair all over your body, which is the body's way of keeping the inner organs warm enough to function. That did it. I started eating again.

Only some years later did "anorexia" become a medical term and diagnosis. Strangely enough, no family member mentioned the fact of me not eating, and no one made mention of it when I started eating again. In our family we did not talk about or question what was really going on with us.

SENIOR BALL, HIGH SCHOOL GRADUATION, AND STARTING TO DRINK

It was Bob's thick black hairy legs showing above his socks that turned me on and prompted me to think of him as a date for the Senior Ball. We sat next to each other in band, blowing into our mouthpieces and jerking the slides of our trombones in and out.

I started playing the alto saxophone when I was in the fifth grade, and switched to the trombone in eighth grade. Music was taught to us starting in the first grade. Why did I start playing the trombone in eighth grade? I liked the shape and the brassy sound of it.

When I was in high school most of my friends went out on dates. Not me, except for my brief adventures with Michael. I wanted to be like my super-confident, flirtatious, and popular girlfriends, but I wasn't. I did not know what to say or how to act with a boy. Maybe this was because I only had sisters? I did not have a strong enough sense of who I was, just my idealistic fantasies, vague yearnings, and newly awakened sexual desires.

As I sat there looking at Bob's hairy legs, I got the idea that probably no one else wanted to go to the Senior Ball with him. Maybe I could ask him, and then my best friend Jane and I could double-date. She was planning to go with her cute apple-cheeked boyfriend. Bob accepted, a bit surprised. He had the dubious reputation of being a suck-up to the teachers, obnoxiously pompous, and "a brain."

My dress was pink and stiff, with a lacey skirt over a satiny underskirt. It was extremely prickly and uncomfortable. How was I supposed to sit down in a skirt like that? A photo shows that my normally straight hair was tightly curled around my face. My costume was complete with high heels that squished my toes together and made me feel unsteady when I walked.

The doorbell rang, and I went and opened the front door. There stood my date in a suit and tie smelling like Old Spice. I let him in. He brought me a corsage and pinned it on me. Pictures were taken by my parents. The car was waiting. Was I really doing this? It all felt so unnatural, so unlike me. I wanted to bolt, but it was too late. I felt a mixture of dread, along with a huge desire to get the evening over with. Bob guided me to the car, and soon we were driving to pick up Jane and her apple-cheeked boyfriend.

I do not remember much of the dance, but I do remember the four of us going out to eat in a fancy restaurant beforehand. Jane obviously did not like my date. She and Bob got into trading snide remarks. Her innocent sweet boyfriend said nothing and neither did I. We just sat there, enduring the uncomfortable situation and being ignored.

How humiliating! This was not fun, sitting there in my stiff pink dress, not saying anything, while the daggers shot back and forth between Jane and Bob. My date was a pompous ass, but that night I wanted to pretend that he was Prince Charming and that I was a beautiful seventeen-year-old girl, full of life and jokes—a happy and lovely Cinderella for a few hours.

After the dance, Bob drove me home. When he stopped the car he said, "We can go as far as you like in regards to sex." I got out of the car, slammed the door and ran up our steps. I never wanted to see him again.

Perhaps it would have turned out better if I'd had something to drink. Shortly after this experience I discovered alcohol.

There were two hundred in our graduating class at Central High School, the oldest high school in Madison. The steps of the brick building were sloped from over a century of students climbing them. We prided ourselves on being the roughest and toughest school in town. The night before the graduation ceremony was our night to get drunk and let it all hang out.

The party took place in the large grassy area in Vilas Park. The park had a zoo with lots of animals in cages, and then there was us, milling around like the animals, but not caged in. The students who owned cars drove the other kids to the park. The cars were loaded down with cases of beer.

We spent several hours wandering around in the dark night, smoking cigarettes, and drowning ourselves in beer. Police cars patrolled the roads around the area, but the cops didn't bother us. They were trained to look the other way. Their role was more like that of chaperones, keeping us out of serious trouble. After all, this was Wisconsin, the dairy state and the beer state. We had a reputation to uphold.

We wandered around for hours, terribly drunk and out of it. After the park scene, about six of us spent the night at one of the girl's homes. I was very drunk, and the next morning came way too soon. Everything hurt and I could not walk straight or think straight. The only thing I didn't do was throw up. (I never have from drinking or I would have quit).

For graduation we had to put on the heavy black cap and gowns. Afterwards we stood bleary-eyed for photos under the blazing hot sun. I squinted in pain, very hung-over.

UW AND THE BEAT DAYS

Marilyn's high school counselor had stupidly recommended that she go to the Stout Institute and major in dietetics. After one year there she came back and enrolled in the UW (University of Wisconsin) in Madison. Back home, we were roommates once again. She entered the journalism school. I spent my freshman year at UW in Integrated Liberal Studies, but followed her path the next year by changing my major to journalism. We took some classes together. I remember a class in European Literature taught by a plump redheaded professor that we both loved.

That's how we happened to be marching up the hill to Bascom Hall in corny green hats and full of green beer. It was St. Patrick's Day. We sang, "When Irish Eyes Are Smiling," and plunked ourselves down in a desk. The kindly professor was Irish and we were studying Irish literature, so we got away with it.

When we weren't physically in class, we hung out in the Rathskellar drinking 3.2% beer, (which was legal on a Wisconsin campus), and smoking cigarettes. Sometimes we went to the library, but mostly we hung out at "the Rat," or at a pizza place on State Street. Sometimes Marilyn and I went to see foreign films at the Majestic theater, then we'd go back to "the Rat." When we got home, we hoped that Mother and Daddy would not notice our unnatural cheerfulness or smell our breath.

In college I seriously worked to change my image again. No more sports, just the required physical education classes at the UW. I let my hair grow long and stringy, wore a trench coat over dark clothes, and smoked filter-tip cigarettes.

Our friends included one very nervous black grad student who was careful not to make any enemies, and another grad student named Enders. He was brilliant, but too giggly and effeminate to be my boyfriend. There was a woman named Judy, plus Marilyn, me, and a few others. We went to parties, but didn't do anything else together except hang out at "the Rat." If it was morning, we drank black coffee and smoked, and later on we drank 3.2% beer and smoked. We fashioned ourselves as part of the rebel "beatnik" movement.

One day, newly arrived in California, I was running across the street in San Francisco, when some guy yelled out of a car window, "Hey, watch out you Beat!" He didn't know what a great compliment he had given me.

PART 2:
EUREKA & THE CASS YEARS

NEWSPAPER REPORTER

When I was about to graduate from the University of Wisconsin I wrote letters to daily newspapers in California. My motto and the motto of my friends was "California or Bust." When I got down to the "E's" I got a job offer from Eureka Newspapers. My friend Jane wanted to be near San Francisco. I accepted the job thinking that Eureka was pretty close to San Francisco. The next day I got a job offer from El Centro in the desert, but my fate was already sealed. I was going to the foggy cold coast.

After writing lots of obituaries and wedding stories, the editor of the paper, Scoop Beale, sent me to the Scotia Inn with a photographer to do a feature story on a woman named Eleanor Holm. He said she was a good friend of his, and he wanted me to do a nice piece on her. This was 1959. I had no idea who this woman was but I figured she must be a celebrity of sorts and I was smart enough to go to the library and look her up in *Who's Who* or some other thick reference book.

A-hah! She was a swimmer! A very good back-stroker on the Olympic team many years before, but she had been thrown off the team by Avery Brundage on the voyage across the Atlantic. She was kicked off for partying with the male athletes. She had been warned, but she had flaunted Brundage, so he kicked her off. This was the Berlin Olympics of 1936. It was a huge scandal.

55

When I met Eleanor Holm, she was sitting nonchalantly in the lobby of the hotel smoking a cigarette. I asked my questions and she answered openly, sometimes laughing at the huge joke of her being thrown off the team for partying when the male athletes partied without censure all the time. It wasn't ladylike for the women athletes—hah! She stubbed out her cigarette. The newspaper photographer took her photo, and he and I drove back to Eureka.

I wrote my story that night. I thought it was pretty good. Eleanor Holm met with Scoop later and said she liked the story. I had been well prepared and asked very good questions. Scoop Beale had tested me and I had passed.

Then I was given the Church Page. One day my friend Jane and I went to an Evangelist meeting. I was writing a feature story on the two visiting pastors. We sat in the church and watched as people were "saved." They rose up from their seats screaming Hallelujahs, and were ushered up to the front. We started to giggle. More people around us got up to be saved. Tears came to our eyes as we choked back our laughter. Then one of the ushers came toward us thinking that we had repented and wanted to join the group of new believers. We shook our heads and stumbled out of the church, deathly afraid that we would be stopped and ushered back down the aisle.

At the newspaper we used typewriters. My copy was always so messy, full of arrows and cross-outs. My fingers have never been coordinated. Scoop sent me to an adult typing class. I had to clean up my act and my copy. I attended the class for about a month and improved my typing just enough to satisfy Scoop, then I quit the class. I'm still a lousy typist.

One of my other assignments was to interview people on the street for our "Question of the Day." I also wrote reviews of plays at Humboldt State College and music reviews of well-known bands that came to Eureka. I started working for the *Humboldt Standard*, an afternoon paper, but eventually I became the Women's Page Editor of the *Humboldt Times*, which was also owned and published by Eureka Newspapers.

It was a veteran reporter named Wally Lee who pushed me to apply for the position. I was happy being a reporter on the *Standard*, but Wally said "This is a chance to move up in your profession." …Huh? I wasn't thinking of moving up in in any profession. When

I was going to college, it was said that girls went to get their "Mrs. Degree." In line with this thinking, I never thought my job on the newspaper would be anything but temporary.

As Women's Page Editor I wrote about the high society of Eureka. One night I covered the New Year's Ball at the Eureka Inn, to which the richest and most powerful people were invited. I had met Cass a few months before, and he came with me. Dancing his jig, he got a little too exuberant and consequently the new women's page editor ended up sliding across the floor on her butt.

One of my wild assignments

It was late in the summer of 1959 when I met Cass. It's a crazy story. My friend Jane's boyfriend was a cowboy/farmer and one day we drove to the hills behind the town to spend the weekend in the family cabin. He had horses that needed to be brought from the wilds to the homestead. I'm not sure why, but I volunteered to ride one of them back to the barn. Jerry was going to ride the other horse. "Yours will just have a halter," he said, "no bridle or saddle."

"No problem," I said, but that wasn't true. Jerry hoisted me up on the horse, who danced and shimmied around, not happy about being ridden after several months of freedom. I should have remembered our palomino Sandy who was obstinate and unbearable when I tried to ride him from one farm to the other at the age of twelve, (my most recent riding experience). With Sandy I was often forced to dismount and lead him down the road.

We set out, Jerry on the horse in the lead, me trying to follow on my steed who was veering sideways, throwing its head, lightly bucking, and very unhappy with my 130 pounds. I was never in control. I laughed a little at the horse's antics. I grabbed tighter to the rope halter and also to the horse's mane. We jerked along, sometimes a bit sideways. Jerry was ahead by a short distance. Then my horse began to trot. I bounced along on its back, grasping the mane tighter saying, "Whoa now, whoooahhh now." The horse then veered to the side of the trail which was lined with trees.

Suddenly the horse began galloping and heading right for a tree with an overhanging limb. I realized the branch would knock me off and that this was the horse's intention. I ducked down but couldn't hang on. Suddenly I was slipping off under the horse, and on the ground. I landed flat on my back. Ow! Then, as I was trying to catch my breath, the horse circled around and started coming back for me at high speed, hooves pounding. I knew I had to get out of its way, but I couldn't move. Somehow, I managed to roll over a few inches, just enough so that the horse's hooves missed me as it went pounding by.

Jerry and Jane carried me to the cabin where I lay the next day doing nothing. I went to the doctor in Eureka when we got home, and he determined from an X-ray that I had crushed a couple of vertebrate. I went back to work a few days later, my torso strapped into a steel brace. My friend Jane bought material which she cut and pinned to the sides of the brace. It looked something like a skirt even though it had no waist. I wore a big bulky sweater over it.

A few weeks later, when I was going slightly berserk from staying in at night, Jerry's sister called and wanted me to go out with her. I agreed with no hesitation. We went to a night club that had a bar and a dance floor. It was a popular hangout. I had my long hair over one eye—Lana Turner style. Two men were sitting at the bar. I saw them flip a coin. A few minutes later the men came over. One of them asked Jerry's sister to dance and the other one asked me. I accepted, but realized that when he put his hands on my back he was going to feel the steel brace.

"I'm not really a cripple," I said. "I broke my back falling off a horse. This is just temporary." He laughed and I relaxed. This man smelled so good and he was very different from my other younger boyfriends. He wore a corduroy jacket. I liked the feel and the smell of the corduroy. I found out he was a fisherman. His friend was a fish buyer.

It was a dark night. He walked me home, and we made a date for the next day. It was Cass. My prince had appeared! The rest is history. If I hadn't gone out that night, if I hadn't broken my back, if Cass hadn't lost the coin toss determining which girl he got, if I hadn't gotten a job offer from Eureka before the one from El Centro, if… if… so many "ifs" bring me to where I am today.

Meeting Cass was a huge turning point in my life. I certainly got a non-conventional man, not a 9 to 5 type guy. Would I have come upon another equally charming, physically active, adventurous, kind of guy? Maybe, because that's the kind of girl I was and that's the kind of man I was looking for.

John Russell Chalmers (Cass) Gidley

After I met Cass I added the waterfront to my beat. I tripped down to the docks in my high heels and skirt to have lunch while working on the newspaper. The smell of diesel, kerosene, fish holds, wet dog, and weathered men was intoxicating.

"Here, have a little wine," one of Cass' friends would say. If I protested that I had to go back to work, "Ah go on. Won't kill you. Make you write better, right Cass?" Or they just set the tumbler full of Dago Red in front of me without asking.

Cass, whose hands looked like a bunch of bananas, cut up hunks of cheese and loaded butter into a cast iron frying pan. When the butter sizzled, he plunked in slices of coarse-looking bread, put the cheese on the bread, and covered it with another piece of bread. The cheese was so thick it came oozing out onto the pan. When both sides were browned, he split the bread open and loaded the insides with tomatoes, onions, lettuce, and lots of mayonnaise. It was a fat-filled and juicy sandwich. When eating it, my fingers got greasy and slippery.

Later Cass drove me back to work in his pickup truck. I wobbled up the stairs in my high heels to the *Humboldt Times and Standard* office feeling warm and happy inside, and a little woozy.

Drinking on the fish boat was my initiation to wine. In the following months I discovered that Cass also liked Scotch on the rocks. He also taught me about Boilermakers and how to make a Manhattan, which was another favorite of his. He told me once that the only thing he would never ever drink again was a Martini. One time at a wedding party he had drunk too many and ended up crawling on all fours, sicker than a dog.

Cass never used a shot glass, he went by the color of the drink. When we went to Cass' sister Mimi's for dinner, Uncle Dick measured out the whiskey. Cass always went back to the bar, grabbed the bottle, and poured an extra amount in his glass and mine. When we went out to a friend's, Cass had the habit of drinking at least one beer beforehand, just in case there would not be enough to drink.

A man who believed in working hard all day and then unwinding with plenty to drink, Cass would fall asleep sometimes while eating dinner. We were married in the oldest, most decorated (with neon lights) chapel in the West in Reno, Nevada. Mimi and Dick were our witnesses. After the ceremony we went out to a dinner show, but Cass fell asleep half-way through dinner.

When Cass found out that he had diabetes (about age seventy-four) he carefully weighed, measured, and monitored his food, and he even quit drinking for a while. Then he must have decided, "Oh, what the hell" because he went back to eating sugar and drinking his Rainier Ale (aka Green Death) until he died.

A buggy load of albacore tuna

Outside our trailer at the Napa Street pier

UNCONVENTIONAL LIFESTYLE

Shortly after I met Cass, my friend Jane moved out to be closer to San Francisco and farther away from her cowboy boyfriend. Eventually Cass and I rented a little house in Eureka. Cass wasn't there a lot. When he wasn't fishing he was driving a semi-truck loaded with crab down to Marin where his crew and son, David, sold them from a dozen crab cookers that he had stationed around the county.

I didn't understand why he didn't park the truck in front of our house in Eureka until he explained that "the bastards are trying to repossess it." Cass also started wearing disguises and using an alias. His full name was John Russell Chalmers Gidley, so he was sometimes John Chalmers, Russell Gidley, J. Gidley, or John Russell. He wore the moustache and glasses that you can buy around Halloween. Cass was forty-six when we met, so there are forty-six other years of stories and incidents that I wasn't part of. As his son from his first marriage said in an article, "Anything illegal, my pop has done it."

Cass always had big plans. I thought of him as "Zorba the Greek," a man who was always moving from one wild scheme and project to the next. I admired that in him. Cass was also a Robin Hood and a champion of the underdog.

One time in Eureka an old veteran newspaperman had been fired due to his drinking. The editor had given him many chances. I felt sorry for the old guy, but I made the mistake of telling Cass. He jumped all over it, accosting my editor as we sat in the bar next to the newspaper office. "What a cruel inhumane thing to do!" Cass didn't even know the old guy, but he still spoke his mind to my boss as I sat there mortified.

When Cass leased a dock in Sausalito I left my job/career, without a moment's hesitation, to live in a tent in someone's backyard in Mill Valley. Cass was starting a commercial fish-buying business. As a fisherman himself, he always accused the fish buyers in the City of rigging the scales and treating the fisherman like dogs. "I want to give the fishermen a fair shake and greet them with a cold beer," he said.

At the dock, I painted buoys, drove fishermen to marine supply stores, and delivered loads of tuna to Fisherman's Wharf. I also did the bookkeeping, although mainly my job was writing out checks, opening bills and statements, making out fish and game tags for the fisherman, stocking the refrigerator with beer, and paying the bills.

The bookkeeping was a pretty haphazard affair. We owed money to lots of individuals and businesses. Cass would pull a name out of a hat to decide who to pay, while I tried to keep the accounts from being turned over to a collection agency.

As the fish-buying business grew, Cass's head blossomed with more big ideas. He envisioned developing a Fisherman's Wharf in Sausalito. Soon we had a beer license, a fish & chips restaurant, a fresh fish market, and a salmon packing plant. Cass's plan was to give the fisherman a beer when they unloaded, but we also gave away fish & chips and more beer than we ever sold in our little restaurant. A cigar box was our cash register.

The salmon-packing plant was built on a weekend with no permits, (in order to foil the building inspector into thinking it had been there for years). It was roughly constructed and painted and Cass told the inspector, "Oh, that building? It's been here all along." The inspector might have taken home a big fat fish for his dinner.

Nuno Tarantino, "a good Dago" in Cass' words, ran the salmon-packing business. I was given the job of salmon slimer. Nuno would take a large salmon and fillet it, then slide it down the watery table to me. My job was to press all the blood out of the fillet with a sharp blade. When the salmon had been filleted and scraped, Nuno and I salted each one down and then packed them into a large barrel. When we had several barrels full, a semi-truck backed down the dock and loaded the barrels. They were shipped back East where the cured fillets were sold as lox.

I was pregnant with Sharon when the salmon season was over, and my job with Nuno ended. I moved back to Eureka to live in a trailer while Cass continued to work in Sausalito. Cass wanted me to apply for unemployment, something I never would have dreamed of doing due to my strict Norwegian upbringing. I applied reluctantly.

On the application, where I was asked to list my latest employment and jobs, I wrote, "women's page editor" for number one, and "salmon slimmer" for number two. The people at the office looked at me with curiosity. There was little chance that they could find a job for me in either of those occupations.

Sharon, aka Froggy, was born on a stormy night. Cass had driven up from Sausalito when I called and said I was having labor pains. The hospital sent me home, however, because I was not dilated enough, so Cass started driving back down 101, a windy highway, in the rain and snow. He had just arrived in Sausalito after a six hour trip, when I called again.

This time labor was for real and I was back at the hospital. I fought off the gas they wanted to give me because I was doing natural childbirth, even though I had neglected to mention that to the doctor. Sharon was born breech. Her little foot had popped out when I had gotten out of the hospital bed to go to the bathroom. Cass declared her name to be Sharon, after the schooner *Sharon*, the only boat that would make it through in such lousy weather.

There is a photo of Sharon at about six-months-old on the schooner. She is being held by Captain Johnny Lund. I have another photo of Sharon, the adult version, perched on the rail of the same boat taken a few years ago when it was in Newport, Oregon. The boat was still a beautiful schooner and Sharon the baby became a beautiful woman.

SHARON

We moved up in the world after Sharon was born. Cass rented us an apartment at the Bon Air Apartments in Greenbrae. We lived there for about four months. Sharon got the nickname "Froggy" from Cass who said her legs kicked out like a frog's when she was an infant in the tub. Cass had a woman accountant in Sausalito who always did his taxes. It was my job at home to sort through all of the receipts and canceled checks and to tabulate them.

Cass usually left early in the morning and I would come to work at the dock later with baby Sharon. In the apartment I kept a large cardboard box full of papers, receipts, cancelled checks—all the stuff I was going through that the accountant needed. The box sat in the living room by the door. One night I had thrown a few newspapers on top of the box before I went to bed.

When I woke up in the morning to start going through more receipts and papers, the box was gone. I called Cass, fearing the worst. I was right. He told me he thought the box was full of old newspapers so he hauled it down to the dock and he and his worker had dumped the contents and the box into the bay that morning.

There was a futile attempt to retrieve them. Cass and a worker went out in a skiff in the fog trying to fish out the papers and receipts. He had to tell his accountant. She was extremely upset, but there was nothing we could do about it. Cass slipped her a nice fat salmon and that was the end of it. I don't know how she got us out of that mess with the IRS.

Soon after I met Cass he bought a twenty-eight-foot Friendship sloop, the *Tia Mia*, with a partner. Later Cass bought out the partner and when Sharon was less than a year old we moved aboard. A friend of Cass' had taken his sailboat to La Paz and raved about the place. As a result, Mexico became our goal. On the first trip offshore away from land, it was Cass, baby Sharon, me, and a three-month-old Airedale named Huckleberry. Both Sharon and Huckleberry wore bright orange life preservers strapped around their torsos. They resembled Tweedledum and Tweedledee. That year we made it as far as San Quintín in Baja before we had to turn back for the opening of the salmon season.

During the years we ran the fish business we had cars, (all junkers and all painted bright yellow), for the fisherman to use. At the end of the day most of the cars ended up at Smitty's, a popular bar on Caledonia Street. The cars were all registered in Cass's mother's name. Somehow no accidents occurred, or maybe the police looked the other way because they got a big fat salmon.

Barbeques and parties on boats abounded. When Froggy was about two years old she sucked her first two fingers. The tops of those fingers were white and puckered with some raw spots. We tried everything, but not even hot sauce would stop her from sucking them.

One night when there was a party on the back deck of a fish boat, Froggy put her fingers into her mouth. I mentioned to one of the fishermen that I couldn't get her to stop sucking her fingers. A weathered old guy pulled his hand out of a pocket. "This is what happened to me when I sucked my fingers," he said. A couple of his digits were missing. Another fisherman showed his hand. "Ya, me too," he said. He was missing a thumb and a finger. Right then and there Sharon's fingers came out of her mouth, for good.

After the season was over, we set off again for Mexico in the *Tia Mia*. Sharon learned how to steer at a tender age and stood a watch. This time we went all the way to La Paz, stopping in at several undiscovered spots on the way down. Cabo San Lucas had only one hotel. Sport fisherman flew in by private plane, the only way to get there. In La Paz there were very few gringo boats in the harbor, a total of about ten. We knew it couldn't last, but I would never have believed that Baja would become the tourist nightmare that it is today.

After our cruise was over, we left the boat on a mooring in front of Jose's shipyard and flew home. The following winter I was pregnant with Lupe and back to La Paz we went.

Drying diapers on the Tia Mia

MY MEXICAN BABY, THE STORY OF LUPE'S BIRTH

I was young and pregnant—you couldn't tell me anything. Warnings from the doctor at the Kaiser clinic that it would be risky to have my baby in Mexico did not dissuade me. The shaking of heads of my relatives and friends, all of whom were opposed to the idea, had no effect on me.

There were good reasons to have the baby there. Our twenty-eight-foot Friendship sloop, the *Tia Mia*, was already down in La Paz. My husband, Cass, and I, (also daughter and dog), had sailed it down the year before and left it there on a mooring in front of José Abaroa's shipyard. It would be cheaper to have the baby in Mexico, and we needed a Mexican citizen for future business purposes.

I also felt that I had the experience and the knowledge to cope with any circumstances. Sharon, who was almost three, was born breech because I was doing Yoga headstands up until the day of her birth. This time I knew better than to stand on my head. I had also just read Pearl S. Buck's *The Good Earth*. The idea was firmly planted in my head that instinct was all that I needed. If necessary, I could "squat in the fields" to have my baby. I was an earth woman.

When I wrote our friends, the Shroyers, and told them that we were coming to La Paz to have the baby, Mary Shroyer wrote back informing us that there was a "new general hospital" in La Paz.

"There's a hospital," I reported to my mother and others who still thought we were a bit daft.

In early December of 1964 we packed up the car and headed south, driving down the mainland to Mazatlán and taking the new ferry across to La Paz. We spent a few weeks in the city, and then we took a cruise up the Sea of Cortez for two months. We arrived back in La Paz on February 15, 1965.

The afternoon of February 16 found me with a giant watermelon-sized stomach, diving off the side of the boat. During the afternoon I had started feeling labor pains, but I didn't want to say anything yet. I had the feeling that this would be my last swim for a while.

I struck out for shore, hauled myself up on the beach, and lay there panting while the workers in the shipyard watched me. After a bit, I waved to them and waddled back out into the water. I set out again for the boat, swimming as gracefully as I could.

Back aboard Cass was barbecuing dorado on the little hibachi. He fixed me our standard Vita and rum drink which I sipped while enjoying the sunset and playing with Sharon. I had a premonition that this would also be my last drink and my last meal and I was determined to enjoy it. After dinner I finally told Cass that I was in labor. By this time it was totally dark and Sharon was asleep in her bunk.

No sooner were the words out of my mouth, than we heard the wind come up. The boat swung around crazily and a beacon of light from the moon splashed down the companionway. There was no need to panic. We had a plan of sorts and just needed to execute it.

The first thing to do was pack up Sharon. She was going to stay with friends on another boat. Huckleberry was fed and instructed to "guard the ship."

The skiff rocked and bounced as we lowered ourselves into it. The moon was full and bright as Cass rowed into the nasty chop. I held Sharon tightly to me, both of us wincing as we were doused with spray. I clung tightly to a scrap of paper in my hand.

I had gone to see a doctor when we arrived in La Paz, but he had been surprised to see me. "You do not understand, doctors do not attend births in La Paz," he said. He also informed us that there was no such thing as prenatal care, and then handed me this scrap of paper with the name and address of a midwife on it.

Senora Lucia Angulo Mendoza Castillo was her name. There was an address on the paper too, but no phone number, (hardly anyone had a phone). The doctor had said that there was no reason to contact the midwife until we needed her services. We were simply to go to the Senora's house when I was in labor and pick her up.

After dropping Sharon off, Cass commenced rowing again, this time for the beach next to the shipyard where our car was parked. It was a tremendous struggle fighting both the wind and a strong cross current, (running about three knots). Despite the fact that Cass was pulling on the oars with all his strength, we barely made headway. Bouncing and slamming into the brightly lit waves, we were being swept downstream.

When we finally made our landfall it was 500 yards down the beach from where our car was. We took our shoes off and walked back up the beach in the water, towing the skiff behind us. I remember how beautiful and eerie the night was with the full moon and the wild wind blowing offshore. Inside me, I felt a turbulence of another sort that was as violent and uncontrollable as the weather. It was surreal.

When we got to the car, Cass asked me if I had the piece of paper with the midwife's name and address on it. Yes, I had it, but neither of us knew exactly how to get there, especially in the dark. We decided that he should drop me off at the hospital first so I could get checked in while he went to find her. Do we have a flashlight, he asked. He rummaged around in the glove compartment.

A couple of months earlier we had driven to the hospital in the daytime to check it out. Stopping the car on the dirt road, we had gazed upon a small flat building that was set back from the road and surrounded by a barbed wire fence. Draped over the fence I saw white things, which I assumed to be sheets, flapping in the breeze. "Looks fine to me," I said. We left the next day to go for our cruise up the Gulf.

Upon finding the flashlight, Cass let me out of the car, and drove off. As I made my way to the front of the hospital I noticed a large population of dogs and cats milling around. At the entrance of the hospital a black dog raised her head and looked at me. Nestled next to her was a litter of squirming black puppies busily nursing.

A horrible thought flashed through my mind. Maybe we had made a mistake and this was a veterinary clinic instead. I pulled and tugged on the door, but it was either locked or stuck. Evidently one did not get sick after hours in La Paz.

It was a chilly night, and I was wearing a thin old red coat. I pulled it around me for both warmth and psychological comfort and tried to figure out what to do next. I was starting to get a little nervous, but it was too late to change my mind about having a baby in Mexico. In one way it felt like time had stopped, in another respect I felt like I was on a roller coaster on a downward track, careening toward a finish line. There was nothing I could do to halt the impending event.

Walking around the side of the building, I saw a barefoot man shuffling toward me. He was dragging a mop, broom, and bucket behind him and I thought he must be a night watchman or janitor. He stopped and slouched up against the building to rest. He lit a cigarette and took in the size of my belly. Wordlessly, he pulled out a ring of keys and motioned me to follow him.

We walked down the outside corridor stopping in front of a double door. He turned to me. "Ahorita," he said making a sign with his thumb and forefinger that he would be back soon, and I was to wait. I feared for the worst, but a few minutes later he reappeared. He was backing out of the door pulling a gurney behind him. On the gurney lay the rigid figure of a man with ashen face and purple lips.

I realized that the man was dead. The watchman maneuvered the gurney next to the building and parked it there. Then he shuffled back and held the door to the hospital open for me.

I had high hopes. Perhaps now I would see the brightly lit sparkling clean white interior of a hospital, and there would be a staff of nurses in starched uniforms to greet me.

When I stepped inside, the first thing that I was aware of was a strong smell of chicken. Two women were huddled together in the bed next to the window, talking and eating from a plate of food on the window sill. A cat jumped in the window and grabbed a chicken bone. Giggling and laughing, the women shooed the cat away.

The only reason that I could think of for them being in the same bed was that they were Siamese twins joined at the hip and that they were going about to have an operation to separate them.

I was directed to the bed next to theirs where there was a large blood stain in the middle of the stripped mattress. There were no sheets. I assumed that the bed was the one recently vacated by the dead man. Lucky me.

The night watchman left. The bed on the other side of mine was empty, but there were rumpled sheets, a blanket, and a pillow on it. Against the wall there were two metal bassinettes, only one with a mattress. The metal ribs on the other one looked cold and uninviting. I was just visualizing my baby in the one with the mattress when a group of people crowded into the room.

Leading the procession was a stooped little old woman dressed in black. She was carrying a tiny bundle and cooing and clucking over it. Several other women swarmed around her, admiring the baby that she held in her arms.

Bringing up the rear, a man wheeled in a woman who was out cold. Mouth gaping open, eyes shut tight, she was hooked up to an IV. A few minutes later the night watchman came in and helped the man lift the woman onto the bed with the sheets.

The man, who I guessed was her husband, stood gazing at the unconscious woman, but no one else paid her any attention. They were too busy fussing over the baby. "Hombre, hombre," they proclaimed, probably happy because it was a boy.

Eventually the baby was laid down in the crib that had the mattress. One by one the women tore themselves away from the crib. They came over to give the unconscious woman a quick kiss, and shake her limp hand, and then all of them, including her husband, left.

It was dark in the room now, and I was conscious of being the only one wide-awake. The two women in the same bed had finished eating. They were lying under a blanket, whispering and dozing. The cat finished the chicken bones, munching and crunching them until they disappeared, and then jumped back out of the window to prowl for food outdoors.

From the bed of the unconscious woman came heavy breathing, accentuated every once in a while by a moan. From the crib came the faint quick breaths of the newborn baby. It was a symphony of frightening life and death sounds.

What was I supposed to do if one of them stopped breathing? Was I in charge of their lives? It was almost as bad as being in labor and being alone.

I pulled my coat tighter around me. What was taking my husband so long? Strangely enough I do not remember any of the pain of being in labor, only the anxiety and the bizarre events of that night.

Just as I had given up hope, the door burst open. I was relieved to see that it was not the night watchman with another patient wanting my bed, it was my husband with the midwife. I was as happy to see her as if she was an angel.

Later Cass told me that trying to find the midwife's house was like navigating in a thick fog. Because there were no street signs in La Paz, he had to stop the car, get out and shine the flashlight on the sides of the buildings. The street names, if they were there at all, were etched into the walls.

The midwife rubbed my stomach and listened to the baby with her ear. I was reassured by her friendly face and no-nonsense manner. After a quick examination she said, "*No es tiempo.*" She said that we should go home and come back later.

"Home?" Row back to the boat? Come back in a few hours? She had no idea what she was asking us to do. My husband used sign language and sound effects to impress upon her what we had gone through. He repeated "*barco, barco*" (one of the few words that he knew in Spanish) and made rowing motions while blowing out like the wind through his mouth. I grabbed her arm and said, "*por favor, no!*" She let us stay.

I was still wearing the red coat with my green plaid maternity dress underneath. She asked us where were the clothes for our baby, where were the diapers, and a blanket? We admitted that we had no clothes, we had no bedding. She looked at us like we were very stupid people to come so unprepared. Then she went out. She came back with a diaper, a shirt, and a thin cotton blanket.

A few hours later when it was "time," she had me walk past the corpse that was in the corridor to another room. I noticed that the plaque above the door read "Cuarto de Expulsion." Expulsion Room, very funny, I thought.

Senora Lucia flipped a switch and the lights came on. She had me climb up on a table and, humming, she made preparations for the delivery while Cass stood nervously in the background.

Somewhere around 4 a.m. the Senora delivered my daughter. She danced around the room with the baby in her arms before laying the dark-eyed new little creature on my stomach. We all cried and laughed with joy and relief.

"She was a wonderful, happy woman, singing the whole time...she literally danced a jig," said Cass when he retold the story of our daughter's birth.

Lucia dressed the baby, singing, and we went back to the room where the baby and I lie on my red coat on top of the bed. Cass went to find us some breakfast. After we ate, he went out again to pick up Sharon and to go look for baby clothes and diapers.

While he was gone, I decided to get up and take a shower. When I came back into the room, there were three unfamiliar women in the room and they were making a fuss over the babies. They were passing my baby back and forth and admiring her fat little cheeks and bright eyes. They wore white smocks and I assumed that they were nurses.

Their job seemed to be of a social and psychological nature. They congratulated me. One of them brought in a chair for me to sit on seeing my bed was now occupied by another person. The night watchman evidently snuck someone in while I was in the bathroom.

When Cass returned, little Sharon came with him, clutching her doll. Cass had baby things and a bright red plastic clothes basket. We laid the baby in the clothes basket and left the hospital.

About 8:30 that morning we arrived down at the beach by Jose's shipyard. The men in the shipyard were just coming to work, and they eyed me again with curiosity. Cass brought José over to view the contents of the red plastic laundry basket. José was astounded, yelling to his workers to come and see.

Soon there was a crowd of men around me and the baby. Yesterday they had seen me swimming off the boat. Today they saw me about to get in the skiff with a new baby and row back out to the boat. This was an unusual feat, even in Mexico.

José scratched his head as we pushed off. He didn't think I should be going out in the skiff so soon. The wind had come up again. We hit some chop, but I was not about to show any discomfort. I smiled back at José and the workers, while my insides bounced painfully up and down.

Looking down on the beautiful face of my new daughter in her plastic laundry basket and at the pert freckled proud face of my other daughter, gave me the guts to keep smiling. I was putting up a front to show that I was one helluva tough woman.

The entire bill for my Mexican daughter's birth, including the cost of the plastic laundry basket, came to $49. My husband Cass, who was always trying to cut down our overhead, bragged about how cheap it was. Having my second child in Mexico was a rousing success. Back on the boat we drank a toast to our Mexican daughter and to the midwife that night.

When it came time to name the baby, we wanted a name that could not be anglicized. I never wanted her to forget her origins or the circumstances of her birth. So we named her "Guadalupe."

My mother-in-law was mortified. "How can you give a poor innocent little thing a name like that?" "

My youngest sister, a teenager in Wisconsin, sent me a flashy homemade card. Fireworks, rainbows, and stars were splashed on the front of the card in loud shades of purple, yellow, pink and orange. On the inside was the message, "Baby, With A Name Like That, You Can Go Anywhere!"

Now, years later, Lupe is a vivacious dark-eyed woman. She does not look like the rest of us, and can she dance!

Baby Guadalupe and our war canoes

WETBACKS

Shortly after Lupe's birth we were on our way home to the good ol' U.S.A. We took the ferry to Mazatlán, then drove up the highway to the border crossing at Tijuana. There were four of us—Cass, me, Froggy, and Lupe in a little plastic clothes basket on the floor of the back seat. Huckleberry, our Airedale, was also in the back seat.

It was a Sunday afternoon and very quiet at the border when we pulled off to show our tourist cards, birth certificates, and smallpox vaccination certificates. The border official told us that there was "a problem." We only had documents for three people. He wanted to know who the dark-haired infant asleep in the plastic clothesbasket was. "That's Guadalupe," Cass said proudly, "she was born in La Paz a few weeks ago."

The man shook his head. He was not going to let us take Lupe into the U.S.! You will have to be cleared by immigration, was what he said. But it was a Sunday and the offices were closed. We pleaded and he finally sent us upstairs to see someone else. We tromped up the stairs with Lupe in her clothesbasket, sat down, and waited.

Did they think we stole a Mexican baby and were trying to smuggle her into the country? Eventually a man in uniform appeared. He asked us many

76

questions about the origins of Lupe. It seems we were supposed to register her birth with the U.S. consulate, (even though there was no such office in all of Baja in those years).

As we were pleading ignorance, Lupe woke up and started making rutting noises. I picked her up. "She's hungry!" The official saw the milk wetting the front of my shirt.

He looked perplexed, but after some deliberations, he stamped a paper. After admonishing us again for not registering her, he sent us on our way. (Luckily it wasn't 2019 when she would have been snatched away from us by Trump's I.C.E. men).

We had another border incident the following year when we inadvertently smuggled fourteen-year-old Urbano into the country. We didn't know, until we were almost at the border, that he didn't have the right papers. By a fluke we were allowed to pass through, even though we had a dark-haired, obviously Mexican boy sitting in the passenger seat.

Our son Memo was born September 29, 1969, in La Paz. When we sailed the *Yo Ho Ho* from Mexico back to the United States in 1970, we didn't make the required stop at U.S. Customs in San Diego because we didn't want to give up our limes, or have to explain who the baby was. That's how at age nine months José Guillermo Gidley de Gartland de La Paz was smuggled into the U.S. and officially became a wetback.

ALL THE PLACES WE LIVED

In the first thirteen years of my life, my family and I lived in the same house on Lakeside Street in Madison. Then we moved to the brick house on the corner lot at 723 South Shore Drive. My mother cried, even though we were only moving a block and a half away.

After I got together with Cass, I never lived in the same place longer than three months. Moving frequently was a lifestyle I got used to. *The Security of Insecurity* was the name of a book popular in the 60's. That was us and how we lived. My first place in Marin County was a tent in Cass's friend's backyard.

Before Sharon was born I lived briefly in a trailer in Eureka while Cass stayed in Sausalito running the fish dock. Then, closer to my due date, we moved to a rental house in Fortuna, a town a few miles away. I was alone a lot of the time and was collecting un-employment. One woman at the unemployment office asked me if I was pregnant, which I quickly denied. In those days you were not allowed to collect unemployment if you were pregnant.

When Sharon was a few months old we moved back to Marin to live in the Bon Air apartments in Greenbrae. Cass had smooth-talked the manager, a woman, into not making us sign a year's lease. We lived there for three months.

After that came the *Tia Mia*, which we sailed to Mexico when Sharon was just under a year old and Huckleberry was a three-month-old Airedale puppy.

When we returned home we moved back into one of the Bon Air apartments. The apartment complex had a pool just down the street. Froggy (aka Sharon) was jumping off and paddling back to grab the side of the pool when she was barely able to walk. The Bon Air apartments were our summer home for a few years.

Another place we lived, this time when Sharon and Lupe were little girls, was Pensacola, Florida in our fold-out Apache tent trailer. The winter of '66 we towed the tent trailer behind the Mercedes to Pensacola where Cass had bought a ninety-eight-foot wooden schooner of the old Red Snapper fleet. He intended to fix it up and do some chartering with it in Mexico. The boat was called the *Carrie B. Welles*, and was immense, with so much rake that Lupe could sit on her tricycle on the bow of the boat, lift up her feet, and coast down the deck to the stern.

The boat was full of cockroaches, which did not make me eager to work on it with Cass. Lupe was still in diapers and we only had the one car, so I stayed in the tent trailer when Cass drove off to work on his boat.

After he went to work, the kids and I would take the bus to the library where I would load up on romance novels and Lupe would run around pulling books off the shelves and babbling, "Baba-ka mi, Baba-ka mi." (Loosely translated, "my book, my book"). The library was cozy and dry inside.

Whoever said it was warm in Florida was not talking about Pensacola. It was freezing and it snowed. After we got back from the library I would hole up in my heavy Indian sweater and my sleeping bag and read. There were state liquor stores where I bought gin to dull my brain and warm my body. There were quite a few kids in the trailer park. An older woman who had a pony and cart gave them all rides.

One day Lupe fell and gashed her eyebrow on the steel corner of the tent trailer and had to be taken to Emergency, but nothing else major happened. We got used to sharing the park bathrooms and I got used to washing our dishes in the bathroom sink. Once I discovered how to get to the library on the bus we were fine. Cass would come back all dirty, hungry, and thirsty, and fall asleep. Then he would get up and leave early the next day for the *Carrie B. Welles.*

We burned up our six-cylinder Mercedes diesel car on the way to Pensacola because Cass had loaded tons of chain and anchors in the tent trailer that we towed behind the car. It was the only new car we ever had. It had red leather seats and was admired by all. Cass took it to a mechanic in Pensacola, but after it was supposedly fixed, there was still something wrong with it. Cass took it back to the shop and when they got it running okay, he decided that we shouldn't have to pay the bill. We left in the middle of the night.

He rousted us up in the dark. We packed in a hurry with flashlights and hit the road. We drove straight through to California in case someone was coming after us to get the money. We drove through New Orleans in the middle of the night. Eerie fingers of fog arose from the tombstones as we drove by the cemeteries next to the road.

Cass had had enough of the *Carrie B. Welles* by then. He abandoned the dream of fixing it up and managed to sell the boat to some guileless young men. The story goes that when they attempted to take it out to sea it started to sink. Luckily, they were able to make it to shore. Several years later two of the men found us down in Mexico and wanted their money back. I doubt if they succeeded because we never had any money.

After living briefly in Florida, we lived the following summer in Tennessee Valley in a falling-down house. Then we moved into the trailer hidden in the bushes by Cass' Marina. It was there that I had a miscarriage.

After I got out of the hospital, the two kids and I lived in a cottage of Cass' friend in Inverness. Then we went back on the boat, then to the rented duplex in Rohnert Park, then to a house on a beach in Mexico, then back on the *Yo Ho Ho,* and then? All the places we went, and things that we did, in the twelve years that we were married are now mixed up in my mind. When did we possibly have time to fit it all in?

I'll attempt to make a list.

1959-61
- Clark St. Eureka
- H St. Eureka
- C St. Eureka
- Tent in Mill Valley

1962
- Trailer Park in Eureka
- Rented House in Fortuna
- Bon Air Apartments
- *Tia Mia*

1963-68
- *Tia Mia* to Mexico
- Back to the Bon Air Apartments
- *Tia Mia*, Sausalito
- Back to the Bon Air Apartments
- The *Yo Ho Ho*
- Tennessee Valley House
- Tent trailer in Pensacola, Florida
- Cass' Marina, trailer in bushes
- Inverness cottage
- Back to the *Yo Ho Ho* (briefly)
- Duplex in Rohnert Park
- Boat skippered from Panama to Sausalito
- *Yo Ho Ho* again

1969-73
- House on beach in La Paz, Mexico
- *Yo Ho Ho* in Mexico
- San Diego on the *Yo Ho Ho*
- Ft. Bragg, Grandma's tent trailer
- *Yo Ho Ho*, Sausalito
- *Amerigo* a boat we skippered from Miami to Seattle
- Hotel in Friday Harbor, WA
- *Yo Ho Ho* again
- The Raft (just me, not the kids or Cass)

1973 (After Cass)
- To the Canal Apartment (2 ½ Years)
- The Blue House (8 Years)
- The Merrydale Apartments (2 Years) Terra Linda

1985 to present
- 128 Belle Avenue, San Rafael (36 years in the same place!)

In the twelve years I was with Cass, we moved thirty times. In the forty-five years after our divorce, I have moved four times. For the last thirty-six years I've lived in the same apartment. After a long period on the waiting list, I began receiving assistance from the Housing Authority. Otherwise, with the cost of rent in Marin, I would have had to move back into a tent.

A birthday card I made for Cass

A WOMAN TRYING TO BREAK FREE

During the years of our marriage, I was continually struggling to become me. I began to feel relief when Cass was delivering a boat or fishing and it was just the kids and me and I could be my own boss. Adding to my restlessness were also the times. It was the late 60's and the early 70's and the hippy culture was flourishing, bringing not only pot and drugs, but also no bras, nudity, communes, open marriages, and alternative lifestyles.

Cass was dead set against the hippy culture, and any other type of lifestyle except the traditional one where the male was dominant with the woman by his side. No gay guys or lesbians allowed. His orientation was all about being straight. Drinking was okay, but pot was not. This seems rather ironic seeing that after our divorce he took the *Yo Ho Ho* on an unsuccessful drug run to Costa Rica on what was supposedly a dolphin filming project.

During the summer of '68 we lived in a ramshackle old house in Tennessee Valley, close to Sausalito. Froggy was starting kindergarten in the fall and Lupe was two years old. It was an unsettling time for Cass and me—we were unhappy together and both having affairs on the side.

The house had steeply sloping floors, rats in the attic, and a duck pond a little way up the hill. We swam nude in the duck pond, listened to Beatle records, and ate pot brownies that my sister Mickey made. Cass ate some too, but he didn't know it. One day we sailed the *Tia Mia* to Tomales Bay and got stoned while Cass worked. On

83

the way back we hit an ebb tide. We stared at the Golden Gate Bridge for hours, feeling that we were going backwards. I think it was partially the current, but mostly the pot.

We had great parties in the house. Cass was in the habit of always inviting people to eat with us, no matter where we lived. One night during a party he stuck the cat up in the attic to take out the rats. We heard loud skirmishes. Everyone cheered when the cat came out unscathed.

We also bought a pony named Dynamite from a neighbor. He had a black and white face. He was not the docile pony you see going around and around in a ring with a child strapped on its back, even though that was his previous role in life.

Living in that house was only temporary. In regard to Cass and me, there was a tension and strain. I found out towards the end of the summer that I was pregnant. We moved out of the falling-down house into the little trailer hidden in the bushes on the side of the dock next to the Marina. The business had expanded from one fiberglass boat to a fleet of about twenty boats of various colors and sizes. I cooked our breakfasts in the Marina office. The kids played on Doo Doo Island, (which was created by Cass and Squeaky Pete dredging the channel in the middle of the night).

One morning in the trailer I started hemorrhaging blood. Almost a bucket full of blood erupted from me. An ambulance tore into the place and sped me to the Marine Hospital in San Francisco where in Emergency they assessed my situation.

For a few days I continued to test positive for pregnancy and I waited, one minute elated that I was still pregnant, the next minute depressed knowing that the little baby inside of me must be dead with all that blood that I had lost.

There was nothing that the doctors could do until the tests finally came back negative. Then I had surgery to remove what they called a "missed abortion."

Psychologically and physically I was a mess. I had lost the baby that was supposed to restore our marriage, and it dropped me into a deep depression. I was in a total tailspin when they sent me "home."

"Home?" Where was that and what was that. I wasn't sure anymore.

I could not go back to the trailer because Cass was going fishing. The girls and I moved temporarily into his sister Mimi's house. She was nice, but after about a week I knew we'd outlived our invitation. Cass was blunt. "What do you want to do?" I resented the question. How did I know? All those years I had been following his plans, his wild dreams, his crazy agenda.

I didn't know what I wanted to do or where I wanted to go. I just knew that I didn't know, and I was depressed.

Eventually Cass came up with a place for us. A friend of his would let us stay in his cottage in Inverness during the winter. The little house was situated in a dark spot among trees. It was wet and cold. For heat, I lit the burners on the gas stove and lit the oven. I took long walks with Lupe in the backpack. Froggy started a new kindergarten there.

I was on a health kick so I fed the kids soy beans mixed with a little peanut butter in their sandwiches, and I mixed bone meal in their juice. Cass drove out to Inverness now and then to see us, but it was no good. I was unhappy with our relationship and wanted to find a new direction for my life.

My epiphany came while living in the little cottage. My son-in-law, who was newly a teacher, turned me on to an inspiring book by Sylvia Ashton Warner about her experiences teaching the Maori children in the Australian bush country. She helped the children discover what they wanted to learn. I ate it up. Being that kind of teacher sounded like such a fantastic and rewarding experience.

Teaching also seemed like a natural choice as a second career for me because I loved learning and I loved kids. I took the first step and sent for an application from Sonoma State College. Then I sent for my transcripts from the University of Wisconsin. A little later, lo and behold, I was accepted. Soon I was going to be a student, working towards a teaching credential.

I moved back aboard the *Yo Ho Ho* with the kids and commuted the 40 miles to Sonoma State. Then, in order to be closer to school, I rented us a duplex in Rohnert Park. Sharon went to first grade and Lupe to childcare (where the teachers were happy to carry her around all day). I loved my classes.

Cass was not happy about us moving off the boat or me going to school, but he was busy working with his charter people to get the *Yo Ho Ho* ready for a cruise to Mexico. He operated like Tom Sawyer. His people paid for the trip, but worked for free first to get the boat ready. I didn't like or trust one of the women who was going on the trip. She struck me as a "Jezebel".

In the meantime, the kids and I were doing fine in Rohnert Park until Christmas vacation came along. I was alone with the kids with almost no money. I bought a scrawny little tree and tried to make a stand out of a tin can, pounding nails into the bottom of the trunk. The tree kept falling over and I gave up, feeling sad and alone.

To make some much-needed extra money Cass was crewing on a friend's fish boat. During the holiday season they would be fishing out of Eureka. He wanted us to come up and join him. I had just enough gas to get there, and of course we went. Cass found us a place to stay, courtesy of another old friend. This time it was an abandoned sawmill, which was his artist friend's studio. Giant hand-carved statues of fierce-looking Indians loomed over us and there was no heat, but it felt good to be a family again.

At night my nose was icy with the cold. The warmest place was inside the sleeping bag with Cass. When I went back to Sonoma State I was pregnant again. I finished the semester and also summer school in order to get my credential, but so much for any teaching job and doing my own thing.

The plan was for me to have another baby in Mexico. The price was right, $49 for Lupe, and she turned out okay. Also, we didn't have a place to live in Marin anymore, not even the trailer hidden in the bushes because we had sold Cass' Marina to Bob and Lois Counts.

Sharon, Lupe, and I would fly down first and get established by renting a house on shore. The *Yo Ho Ho* was supposed to arrive before the end of September, which was my due date, but I should have known not to count on it. Memo was born September 29, but Cass and the *Yo Ho Ho* didn't arrive until February of the following year.

The Yo Ho Ho—54' Alden cutter

Froggy climbing the rigging

TO MEXICO BEFORE MEMO

In August, the two kids and I, along with two huge packing boxes of household goods, flew to San Diego where Marilyn and her husband Frank, and their young baby were living. After visiting them we were going to fly from Tijuana to La Paz. A good friend, Mary Shroyer, would help us find a place to rent until the boat arrived. I was eight months pregnant and as big as a house.

We spent a few days in San Diego, then Frank loaded us up and drove us to the airport in Tijuana. We got the boxes through customs with the help of some dinero crossing the palms of some officials. We were waiting to board the DC-3 prop plane when an employee came up and said that the captain was refusing to fly me unless I had a medical clearance from a Mexican doctor. He was not joking.

My brother-in-law reloaded the huge packing boxes, which contained clothes, toys, books and a sewing machine, back into his pickup and drove us around Tijuana looking for an office with a "medico" sign that was open on a Saturday afternoon. We finally succeeded. I passed the quick physical and the doctor signed the paper that I was fit to go, (although we had missed the one daily flight to La Paz).

Frank drove us back to San Diego. My sister Marilyn and the baby were taking a nap. When we left that morning she was probably relieved to be alone, and there we were again. "Surprise," I said.

The next day, the official medical clearance in hand, we went back to the airport. We paid *mordida* again to get the boxes through customs, and then, whew, the girls and I were on the plane. We settled in, but our relief was short-lived.

When we landed in La Paz, the kids and I were dying to get off the plane. Then the door opened. The heat that hit us was intense. It was a furnace out there. I did not think it possible that people could live in that heat. I wanted to reconsider and go back, but the door of the plane was closing behind me.

Well, here we go on another adventure, I thought.

Our baggage was loaded into a taxi, and we started to drive around looking for Mary Shroyer. She and I weren't clear on where we would meet and there were no cell phones, not even any regular phones, and no air-conditioning in the cab. I knew vaguely where she lived, but didn't know how to get there. The taxi driver was happy to drive us around town on the mostly dirt roads looking for her.

Suddenly I saw Mary Shroyer bouncing along the road in her jeep and kicking up an immense cloud of sand and dust. She and her two little boys jumped out to greet us.

We arrived at her house dirty, tired, and sweaty. She graciously showed me a cot in the yard that I could sleep on and a large water tank that we could cool off in. I eased my blimp of a self into the tank. She made me a drink. The water felt so good! I had dreams of staying in it forever, sipping frosty margaritas, and drinking ice cold beer.

Mamacita Lupe and Memo

THE HOUSE BY THE BEACH IN LA PAZ

The house that Mary Shroyer found for us was on the outskirts of town by the bay of La Paz—a perfect location on the beach. I liked the palm trees in the large front yard and having no neighbors nearby. The only sign of human activity was a dirt road winding around the front of the house. I didn't know that the road led to a cement plant and a parade of trucks would drive back and forth day and night.

It was so unbearably hot in my bedroom that I decided to sleep on a cot in the yard. Sharon and Lupe, ages seven and four, were okay in the house. I checked on them before I went out to the yard. They had beads of sweat on their brows, and their hair was so damp that it stuck to their faces.

I slept nude with only a sheet to pull over me when the blinding lights from one of the trucks came around the corner. I cowered underneath my sheet. The trucks were noisy and kicked up clouds of dust. Their huge headlights lit up the particles of dirt in yellowish, grayish, brownish clouds as they rumbled by.

Another problem that prevented a good night's sleep was the bugs. I kept a flashlight and about a dozen different bug sprays and insect repellents lined up under the cot to fight the mosquitos, spiders, flies, and no-see-ems that attacked me during night. An eight month pregnant female with a big belly and juicy white skin must have been a real treat for them. Finally, after Memo was born, I got a small air-conditioning unit for my bedroom window and slept inside with him.

Soon after moving into the house, I enrolled Sharon and Lupe in the public school, which was within walking distance from our house. It turned out that there were a lot of people living in small cement houses and shacks not too far from us. All the kids in that neighborhood went to the same school and when they got to know us, all the kids came to our house and yard to play.

Sharon was originally put in the first grade because she didn't know any Spanish, and Lupe, only four, was in the second year of "Kinder." (In Mexico, children went to Kindergarten at ages three, four, and five). After a few weeks of playing with the amigos and amigas, Sharon picked up enough Spanish so they moved her into second grade. By the end of the school year Sharon had straight A's on her report card and was a whiz at jumping rope.

One day all the kids came running into my bedroom screaming, "*Alacran, alacran!*" I wasn't familiar with the word or the terror that it was causing in the room they were playing in. I carefully peered under the chair where the children pointed. I saw nothing, but I found out later that *alacran* means scorpion in English. In La Paz they are jumbo-sized and have a lethal sting.

Scorpions were only one of many creatures that I became familiar with. We had a friend from Marin staying who thought a giant black spider over the doorway was a Halloween decoration. Oh, no! It was as large as a frying pan, but it was real. We were also overrun with cucarachas, mainly in the kitchen and the bathroom. At night they came up the shower drain and scurried into the kitchen where they hid out in the cupboards. Mary Shroyer gave me a tip.

"Put a cap from a peanut butter jar over the drain at night," she said. I followed her advice. During the night we would hear plenty of racket. The cucarachas would be rattling the lids as they tried to push them up and get in, which they still managed to do.

Our house by the beach began to feel a lot more like home after Huckleberry, the dog, and LeRoy, the cat, arrived. They were flown together in a specially made plywood box. Before we left Sausalito, I had painted a crude portrait of Huckleberry in green paint on one side of the box, and had I written both their names on the other side of the box. The custom officials at the airport in La Paz scratched their heads when they saw a dog and a cat jump out of the same box.

Huckleberry was a big hit with everybody in Mexico and had a happy time, although LeRoy suffered an unhappy ending. I write about it in "The Tale of LeRoy," a story at the end of this book.

Housework in La Paz included dusting every piece of furniture, sweeping and mopping all the floors, washing clothes and diapers, and shopping and cooking. Fortunately, I didn't have to do most of it. We had the help of Huera and her sister Lupe who lived in the neighborhood. The clothes were hand-washed on a large stone structure in the yard. The dirty clothes were scrubbed clean on the bumpy surface of the wash table, then rinsed with water from the hose and hung up to dry. Our clothes had never looked so clean or smelled so good.

A scary time occurred when Memo was about three weeks old. He was still pooping green watery poop and not gaining weight. The doctor in the military clinic told me that it was normal. I wasn't sure I believed him. Then one afternoon I started hemorrhaging blood. That night I walked the kids down the beach to La Posasda hotel, which was the closest place that had a telephone. I called the long distance operator and then we sat down to wait until she called me back with a connection. I told Cass I needed to fly Memo and myself up for medical treatment.

Mary Shroyer took Sharon and Lupe, and Memo and I flew up the next day. When we saw a doctor in Sausalito it turned out that Memo had salmonella, and my hemorrhaging was caused by a piece of the placenta that was stuck inside me. Cass and crew were working on the *Yo Ho Ho*, but it was not ready to sail. After treatment and a few days Memo and I were well enough to go back to La Paz.

A little later there was another medical crisis. Memo developed pneumonia when he was a few months old. I took him to a gringa nurse that I knew in La Paz. She filled a giant needle that looked longer that Memo's tiny butt and proceeded to inject him with penicillin. Memo was probably too young to remember the shot.

Lupe, however, will never forget an injection that she was given in "Kinder." I don't remember any permission slip being sent home. Lupe says that on the day of the shot, the teachers and aides danced the kids one by one into a special room. When they came out, the kids were crying so Lupe knew something was wrong. The shot they were getting was a TB vaccination, (not the test), and it was injected straight into a child's shoulder. The good thing is that Lupe will never get TB, but she does still have a scar on her shoulder, and a painful memory.

In Mexico, we also experienced ringworm, impetigo, scabies, bed bugs, and head lice. Usually I coped with these problems alone, but Cass was around for the head lice problem. His treatment was to submerge our heads in a bucket of sheep dip, (used for de-licing sheep—why not humans?) Although my head felt like it was on fire, my hair didn't fall out, and it got rid of the lice.

Another reason to bring the *Yo Ho Ho* to Mexico was Cass thinking that we could start a charter business down there. This never happened, partly because the Mexican government was cracking down on gringos who were chartering their boats. It seemed a bit risky, even though now we had two Mexican citizens. The authorities had recently impounded a diving boat owned by an American, even though he had a Mexican wife.

My friend Tam came to live with us in the La Paz house before Cass and the *Yo Ho Ho* arrived. We didn't lack for parties and entertainment. In the evening we played horseshoes in the side yard and drank gallons of rum mixed with Vita Toronja. Mac and Mary Shroyer came to the parties, and Peeky Douglas, and other boat friends, and friends of friends. All the neighborhood kids came too, accompanied by their big dogs. They played with Sharon and Lupe in the Rec room or ran around in the yard. The Mexican children drew colorful pictures of little houses, palm trees, sun, and blue skies, and the pictures that Sharon and Lupe drew looked just like theirs.

In February of 1970, the *Yo Ho Ho* finally arrived. The people who came off the boat were invited to come into the house to take a shower and to eat meals with us. They slept on the boat. One morning when I was nursing Memo in the bedroom, the "Jezebel" woman came in to take her shower. A little later I heard Cass outside the shower window whispering, "Buenos días." Then I heard the woman's, "Buenos días, mi amor," back to him. I couldn't ignore what I had already suspected.

I angrily accused Cass of sleeping with her, but he denied it. I didn't know what to do. I was far from home in Mexico, with a baby and two other kids, and no money of my own. After the woman and the rest of the guests flew home, things settled down again and I let it go. But I wasn't rid of her yet.

DEAD BABY RABBITS

We sailed the *Yo Ho Ho* back up the coast from Mexico that summer, headed for "home." But when we stopped in San Diego, we heard that the weather was terrible in Marin, while it was calm and sunny where we were. I agreed that there was no hurry. We should stay in San Diego. We anchored out near the yacht club staying there for almost a year.

Sharon was reluctant to start school in San Diego. "The farther south you go, the tougher they get," she said. I finally coaxed or bribed her into going. She was in third grade and Lupe in kindergarten. Memo was not quite a year old. One day I was invited by the women of the yacht club to sail our dinghy in a race. Memo fell asleep in the bottom of the boat, but we won the race.

Soon Cass decided to go back fishing. He bought a fish boat and called it the *Wayfarer II*. The *Wayfarer I* had sunk on him years before. *Wayfarer II* was destined to sink also, or at least that was the plan, but that's another story. (I wrote a screenplay and a short story based on it).

He and some Mexicans, brought up illegally, were working on the boat in Ft. Bragg. We joined him for part of the summer. Cass found a place in the woods at the end of Simpson Lane for myself and the kids. A woman named Gramma lived on the property. Her daughter and son-in-law, who were Cass's friends, lived in a house just up the hill from where we camped.

Gramma had a trailer that we could use and we brought our tent trailer up to make more room for sleeping. Memo was a white-haired, barely walking little toddler. Cass bought him a pair of leather work boots that were too large for his feet, but he strutted around happily with his diaper hanging down to his knees.

Memo and I slept in the trailer and Froggy and Lupe slept in the tent trailer. Outdoors there was a swing, lots of trees and grass, and a big mama rabbit in a cage that Gramma said was pregnant.

Gramma was going on a trip and wouldn't be back until after the babies were born. She said that rabbits have huge litters. "No problem," I said. Gramma told me approximately when the babies were due. I would need to put a couple of layers of newspaper on the floor of the cage. Otherwise the tiny rabbits would fall through the wire bottom.

Around the 4th of July, there was a parade in downtown Ft. Bragg. Memo had a fever and I wasn't sure we should go, but the kids wanted to. During the parade I held Memo. He felt so hot, his cheeks, his legs, and his arms were burning up.

That night when I carried him into the trailer to go to sleep I flashed upon my sister Patty going into convulsions and the panic that surrounded that event. I remembered my mother and father snatching her up and putting her in the kitchen sink. I remembered how her eyes had rolled back in her head.

In the very next moment, Memo, lying in bed next to me, went into convulsions. He turned limp and blue and his eyes rolled back in his head. I jumped up and grabbed him. There was a small bathtub in the trailer, but the water came out in a thin orange stream. I sat in the narrow little tub holding Memo in my arms and screamed for Sharon to go up to get our neighbors, Eleanor and Dan. She ran up the hill in the dark.

The woman named Eleanor was talking non-stop as she drove us to the hospital. I couldn't hear a word that she said. I was holding the limp lifeless body of my son in my lap, wanting her to drive faster and shut up.

In the hospital Memo was examined. He came to life again, and the doctors told me he was going to be okay. I was relieved and thankful. I took him home. I understand now that convulsions are nature's way of preserving the brain when someone has an extremely high fever, but it is scary to see. If a child goes into convulsions, you will think the child is dead.

The next day Memo was a happy little guy again as he strutted around in his too-big work boots with his diaper hanging around his knees. I took him down to see the noisy Skunk train come steaming into the station. He loved that train. I was so relieved that he was alive and well, I would have done anything for him—anything.

Cass and Memo on Wayfarer II

One night towards the end of the summer we had a wild party. I can't remember who was there but we were doing a lot of drinking. I forgot about Mama Rabbit and the prospective babies. I didn't check her so I didn't put any newspaper down. I weaved my way to bed, even though in the back of my mind I knew that their births were imminent.

The next morning, I woke up with a hangover, feeling very bad. Suddenly I remembered the rabbits. I stumbled outside to Mama Rabbit's cage, and there they were—hundreds of tiny white corpses. Most of the baby rabbits had fallen through the wire and lay scattered about on the ground. Other babies were hanging half in and half out of the cage.

Mama Rabbit did not seem concerned, but I hated myself. I picked the dead babies up with a shovel and carried them to a remote corner of the garden. I dug a mass grave and buried them all before the kids got up. It didn't console me much that Gramma raised rabbits in order to eat them.

I took the kids on a hike by the ocean to try to cleanse myself, but the horrid sight of the dead little rabbit babies kept coming to mind. I decided there would be no more drinking. *You can't drink anymore because this is what happens!* I was terribly ashamed and still sick with the hangover.

When Gramma came back she wondered how Mama Rabbit had gone from being pregnant to not being pregnant without there being any babies. We were busy packing up and getting ready to leave. I acted dumb and shrugged my shoulders. We left Ft. Bragg before she pressed me to explain further.

ANCHOR-OUTS

We went back to San Diego and the following summer we sailed the *Yo Ho Ho* to Sausalito and anchored out near the Napa Street pier. Cass was fishing fulltime on the *Wayfarer II*.

In Sausalito I was rowing the kids, the dog, the groceries, and fresh water back and forth from the dock to the boat. We were in dire need of money when miraculously Cass got a job delivering a big cruiser, the *Amerigo*, for the new owner who lived in the East Bay. The boat was in Miami. After leaving Florida, the boat would travel through the Caribbean and the Panama Canal, up the coast of Central America and Mexico, all the way to San Francisco. The owner's family would be aboard.

Cass informed them that I would go as cook. At first the owner said that Memo could come with me, but then the grandma balked. She didn't want a "baby" on board. I had already lined up Patty and Jon, my sister and brother-in-law, to move aboard the *Yo Ho Ho* which was anchored out, to take care of Lupe and Sharon.

They agreed to rowing the girls back and forth to school, shopping on shore, cooking the meals, hauling the water and groceries, and rowing the kids back to the boat. But they couldn't take on Memo too. I needed to find someone to take him right away.

I wracked my brain. Not Mimi and Dick, Cass' sister and brother-in-law, who lived in a nice house, always clean and neat, like themselves. Another friend was splitting up with her husband so she wouldn't be able to take him. Then I thought of Tam. I had met her at Sonoma State where we were both pursuing teaching credentials the year before Memo was born. She was single and lived in Mill Valley and she was a good friend.

"That's what friends are for," she said, "but I can do it only if he is in school or has some place to go during the day." I thumbed through the phone book and called around. Most places said he was too young for their child care programs. "He has to be at least two years and eight months," said the woman on the phone at the Presbyterian Church in San Rafael.

The next day I called back, changing my voice slightly. "When is his birthday?" a different woman asked me. I told her that he was born June 29. "Ok, he is just barely old enough, but you will have to bring him in for a trial to see if he can adjust."

I was a little apprehensive because Memo had always been a bit of a clinger. The next day I led him by the hand into a colorfully decorated room with tiny chairs where it was a little noisy and there were lots of busy little kids. Suddenly he jerked his hand out of mine and went running to the far side of the room where some little boys were making engine noises and playing with toy cars. He never looked back.

"It looks like he will do just fine," said the teacher.

Whew, he passed, and I only lied a little bit about his age. Although everything went fine that day, Tam reported that he almost flunked out later, clinging to her legs and crying when she was dropping him off. But by that time I was already in Florida on the boat.

The *Amerigo* was delivered without mishap although it took longer than expected. Instead of three months it was about five months. When I came to pick Memo up he would have nothing to do with me. "Take a bath," "Molina Park," and "ice cream," he said. Tam explained how these activities kept him happy. He hid under Tam's table and cried when I pulled him out. I carried him screaming to the car.

Back in Sausalito Cass was still working on his fish boat and I was back on the *Yo Ho Ho* with the kids. In order to keep Memo in daycare, I needed to get a job. My sister Patty saw a newspaper ad that waitresses were needed for the new Howard Johnson's restaurant opening on Shoreline Highway between Sausalito and Mill Valley. Patty and I applied and both of us were hired.

HO-JO'S (AKA HOWARD JOHNSON'S)

When Patty and I started working at Ho Jo's we went through two weeks of intensive training. At the end of the training we were given name tags, little green aprons, and a green and white checkered uniform. My sister and I were going to be a waitress.

I could keep Memo in daycare, the one in Marin City. I could get off the boat during the day and have a place to go. Life was looking brighter. I opened up my own checking account, Cass did not understand why, but I knew why. It meant my own money, plenty of coins for the Laundromat, and nobody's name in the hat.

At $3.08 an hour, plus tips up to $20-$30 on a good day, I was rich! When I worked the early shift, a cook made Memo hotcakes shaped like animals, then walked him over to the daycare center. When I picked Memo up after his long day at daycare, I would stop at the supermarket to shop for groceries. I would feel guilty and buy him a cheap little toy. If I didn't buy him a toy, he would have a fit in the store and scream his head off.

Ho Jo's gave me a taste of the corporate world in which district managers get paid to make very important decisions like whether the salt and pepper shakers should go on the right or left side of the advertising "tents" on the table. Nothing was ever done to improve the lives of us waitresses, such as adding a busboy to a shift.

When I was in high school, I had worked as a carhop at the A&W Root Beer stand near our house on South Shore Drive. My experiences resulted in some bad dreams. In one of them I am carrying a tray of heavy root beer mugs and food, but I can't find the right car. I wander around going from car to car in the dark. I eventually trip and drop the tray. The heavy glass mugs shatter into pieces splattering root beer all over me.

After Ho Jo's, I had waitress dreams that persisted for many years. Usually there were too many people coming in the door of the restaurant. They are waiting to be served and getting impatient. I can't take care of them all. There's not enough help. This was often a reality, not just a dream.

The restaurant had many problems like running out of bread when a busload of Canadian tourists stopped in for tea and toast, or not having any soap for the dishwasher. Fleas were everywhere. Patty sewed flea collars in the hem of her uniform to keep the fleas from eating her legs alive.

A mouse that someone caught was put in a large glass jar and sat on the manager's desk. If food had fallen on the floor before we delivered it, the cook would scoop it up and realign it on the plate. One time the assistant manager and the cook started fighting behind the counter. We waitresses kept on working despite their scuffle.

At Ho Jo's we were a community of characters. We drank together after work and partied together. The women formed a softball team. My kids and my friend's kids were cheerleaders at our games. I worked at Howard Johnson's for a total of five years, although the last three of those years I was part-time. I used to say I earned my master's degree in waitressing.

Santiago found me at Ho Jo's in 1973. When he spread his raft plans out on the table in a booth, I was ready to go.

The raft participants—I'm fourth from the left

THE ACALI

There was another reason I wanted to get away and drift across the Atlantic Ocean, and it had to do with Cass. One night in late October I had leaped off the bow of the *Yo Ho Ho* and swum ashore in my clothes to escape his wrath. He had overheard me revealing my true feelings to a friend about our relationship and talking about the other man I was seeing.

I stupidly let him row my friend back to the dock. When he came back to the boat he started drinking and alternately choking me and banging my head against the bulkhead. He demanded to know who the other man was. I felt like my life was going to be over. He was going to kill me.

After a couple of hours Cass was very drunk. I managed to get up the companionway and out on deck and into the skiff. But, before I could get it untied, he got in after me. There was a struggle. When he grabbed my arm I wrestled it out of the sleeve of my Indian sweater and scrambled back up on deck. I ran to the bow of the *Yo Ho Ho,* jumped off, and swam for my life.

After slogging my way through the mud at low tide, I made my way to the 7-Eleven across Bridgeway Avenue. Then I called Patty to come get me. It took Cass' violent behavior to motivate me to file for the divorce.

✧

In 1973 divorce proceedings were underway. The kids and I were still living on the *Yo Ho Ho* while I looked for an apartment to rent. One day at Howard Johnson's, I got a phone call from a Mexican named Santiago Genovés. He was looking for a female captain and navigator to lead an experiment that involved drifting across the Atlantic Ocean on a raft. His friend in San Francisco got my name through my navigation instructor.

Santiago's plan was for women to be in the commanding roles while the men would cook, clean, and take photos. *Well, that sure sounds interesting, but not at this time in my life.* That very day I had signed a lease for an apartment in San Rafael. I said no to Santiago.

The next day Santiago came into the restaurant with the plans and spread them out in a booth. "I can't sit down in a booth with my uniform on, or I'll be fired," I said. He was persistent. I sat down and looked at the plans. I was impressed by how solid and seaworthy the raft would be, with huge steel pontoons under the water to give it stability.

Cass surprised me by being all for it. He thought I could come back and write about it and make a lot of money. I could hire a live-in babysitter when it came time to move into the apartment that I had just rented. He would check in on the kids from time to time when he wasn't fishing. Memo was three and a half years old, Lupe was eight, and Sharon was eleven.

I was also thinking a few months away might cool Cass' anger towards me. If I was at sea he wouldn't be able to harass or threaten me in the months before the divorce became final.

On the plane on my way to Spain, I noticed how vast the ocean was beneath us. It was going to take us twenty hours to get there, and we were going to <u>drift</u> back? *How crazy was that? What had I done?* It didn't bother me for long though, because I still had the blind faith that everything in my life would turn out fine. This experience was meant to be, and I was going to have an adventure all my own.

It was later, when I was already in Spain, that Cass turned against Santiago and the raft. He found out that the participants would not only be leaving their spouses and children behind, but were also expected to establish new intimate relationships on the raft, in line with the "open marriage" idea of the late 60's and early 70's. It also didn't help that the international press wrote sensational stories dubbing us "The Sex Raft" and "The Raft of Passion."

When we first arrived in Spain we were housed in a monastery in Madrid. After a few weeks of testing our physical, mental and emotional health, our IQ, and our handwriting, we were flown to the Canary Islands off the coast of Africa where the raft was to be outfitted. We were put up in a hotel overlooking a beach that was crowded with tourists, but we did not have any time to play. The raft needed a lot of work and the hurricane season would be coming to the Caribbean. We worked another three weeks to get the raft ready.

There were eleven of us in the international crew, six women and five men. Santiago at age forty-eight was the oldest. He had drifted on a raft before with Thor Heyerdahl of *Kon Tiki* fame. Maria, our captain, was thirty-two years old and from Sweden. She and I (and Santiago) were the only ones who had spent any time at sea. I was thirty-five at the time. Santiago planned for us to be from different cultures and backgrounds and even speak different languages. One of the five men was a black Catholic priest from Angola. There was an Israeli woman and an Arab woman, a black woman from the U.S., and a white one—me.

Finally, on May 17, 1973, we were towed out to sea and dropped into the current to begin the long voyage home. The expedition was almost aborted when Olaf, Maria's fiancé who was on the tow boat, decided that Santiago was "a madman" and unfit to lead, and ordered Maria off the raft. After some angry exchanges back and forth in Swedish, Maria decided to go, in spite of Olaf.

Because Santiago didn't want us to be entertained, we had no books, radios, or music of our own on the *Acali*. Two books written by Santiago were allowed, Bowditch's book on seamanship, one small guitar, and that was it. We also were not supposed to bring cigarettes or alcohol, although Maria smuggled some Scotch aboard and Charles brought several cartons of cigarettes.

Once underway, it was not all smooth sailing. Shortly after leaving we started seeing sharks following us. That ended our bathing, which we had been doing while tied to a line behind the raft. Almost immediately Santiago also began berating us for not having any conflicts and not making any intimate relationships. He wanted something newsworthy to report to the world over our radio. Throughout the journey he kept complaining, "you are too much in your own little shoes."

Maybe to initiate some conflict Santiago started singling out some of the crew for his disapproval. First it was Rachida, then Edna, then Maria, then Charles, then Eisuke...I can't remember what Rachida or Charles did to anger him, but he berated Edna, the nurse, for shaving her legs and for not bringing any Band-Aids along. Maria was censured because she wrote in one of the questionnaire's that she "hated the raft." Eisuke, the photographer, and Santiago were at odds because Eisuke didn't want Santiago telling him who to film and who to take photos of. He also didn't like Santiago sleeping with a certain participant.

In the Atlantic the rudders broke twice, but they were repaired underway. Seeing we were drifting, it wouldn't have mattered much. The scariest moment happened in the Caribbean, when we almost got run over by a freighter. It was early in the morning and the freighter was heading right for us. At the last minute they saw the flares I was shooting up and turned away, but it was a very close call.

We also sailed into the tail-end of a hurricane. Edna got lashed across the neck with a slapping line, but no one else was injured. The wind screamed and the rain pelted us fiercely that night. The next morning, after all was quiet and sunny again, Maria and I observed that the raft had been turned completely around, and we were facing the wrong direction!

When we started out, Maria was the captain of the raft. Santiago said his dual role was leader of the expedition and also a participant in the experiments. But after we left Barbados, Santiago said he no longer had confidence in Maria, and from then on, he was the captain.

Two factions developed on the raft—the three participants who supported Santiago, and the rest of us who were rebellious and still supported Maria as captain.

When we got to Barbados there was also the question about whether we should continue to Cozumel. We were late leaving the Canary Islands and, as a result, would be going through the Caribbean during hurricane season. Another consideration was that the *Acali* expedition was financed by the Mexican government. I heard that Santiago's wife told him he would be "the laughing-stock of Mexico" if he didn't continue.

Finally, after 101 days we arrived in Cozumel looking scraggly and dirty, except for Santiago. He managed to pull out brand new, clean white trunks from under his floorboard. After that he would not sit on the raft unless a towel was placed down first. When we neared the shore there was a flotilla of boats and yachts, thousands of people, mariachi bands, and fireworks to greet us. Frankly, after being at sea for so long, all these people and all this attention and noise was frightening.

Santiago hustled us off through the crowds and into vans that took us to a motel where we were debriefed for the next five days. We were not allowed to talk to other people or to go anywhere until the debriefing was complete.

During our sessions all the bad feelings toward Santiago came out. Maria likened him to a "man of the Gestapo." Eisuke, our Japanese photographer, wanted to shove him overboard. At a press conference, when a newsman asked Maria about the sex on the raft she said, "There was none of that. I did not see or hear of any sex on the raft." This was not exactly what the press wanted to hear.

There was some difficulty in collecting the money due us from Santiago. The Mexican government and its Channel 13 were the ones who paid for the raft and our participation. I told a reporter that we were not going to leave Mexico City unless paid what was promised and that we were prepared to camp on Santiago's lawn until we got our money. A few days later we got paid and I flew home.

Abruptly I was dropped back into civilization where I took up my role as a single mother. The divorce had become final one day in July when the raft was halfway across the ocean. I was home now and having to deal with the reality of living in an apartment with three children to take care of and a not so glamourous job as a waitress at Howard Johnson's.

On the raft, we had only the few bottles of whiskey that Maria had smuggled aboard and some cooking wine. At home I started feeling depressed and started drinking more. I saw a therapist who said I was medicating myself with wine and that I needed to go to AA before any therapy would help me. She also noted that I was "drifting off" as I talked to her and that I wasn't finishing my sentences—a symptom of my depression and lack of direction.

I reluctantly went to my first AA meeting. Actually, it was my second because when Marilyn and I were studying journalism we were sent to do a story on an AA meeting. How ironic! Both of us would end up there years later to tell our stories.

The Raft

PART 3: MID-LIFE

Ta-daaaa! Lupe, Sharon, Memo, and friends

THE CANAL

When the kids and I moved off the *Yo Ho Ho* and I was back from the raft, we lived in the Canal area of San Rafael. The neighborhood consisted of rental apartments of mostly single mothers with kids. Lupe and Sharon had many friends. They came and went freely from one apartment to another and swam in the pool that served two of the buildings. They played in the marsh and walked to school. The kids were pretty much on their own, and we moms were free too.

For me, who had been living anchored out on the *Yo Ho Ho*, moving into the apartment was a huge step up. I was content to sprawl out on the wall to wall carpeting. Who needed furniture? All I needed to do was buy a vacuum in order to vacuum the rug, which I did in 1973, (and it still works in 2019).

In the apartment there was hot and cold running water, electricity, a garbage disposal, a shower and a tub. I didn't have to row ashore to get in my car. I just had to walk out the door to the carport.

We lived two and a half years in the apartment in the Canal—me working at Howard Johnson's, the kids in grade school, and Memo still going to daycare in Sausalito. I wasn't that happy being a waitress again, but it was difficult to give up all that tip money. I always had cash in my pocket, and the excess I stuffed in my top dresser drawer.

The day came, however, that our landlords decided to sell our building. He and his wife asked if the realtors could have a look inside the apartment. I agreed and went off to work. A few days later I looked in my dresser drawer for all my tip money. The pile of mostly one dollar bills that I'd been saving were gone. There was no money. I was positive that the real estate agents had taken the money out my drawer on their walk through the building.

The landlords had been outside working on the grounds when the team of real estate agents went through my apartment. I was so sure that they had taken my money that I filed a claim in Small Claims Court. All of the real estate agents, as well as my landlords, were summoned to appear.

In court, none of them admitted to have stolen my money, although one woman realtor commented that my apartment was "so messy nobody could have found anything in there." The judge stuck up for me. "Thank you, but we are not here to judge Mrs. Gidley's housekeeping abilities."

The verdict came after a few days and I had lost. Since I'd given my landlords permission to let the agents in, it didn't matter that they had been working outside at the time. I was unhappy about the outcome, but at least I tried.

Several days later I needed something on the top shelf of my closet. I stood on tip-toe and swept my hand up high to dislodge it. Suddenly a shoebox came careening down and money began raining down on my head. It was my tip money! I didn't tell anyone because I felt too embarrassed. I didn't remember putting the bills in the shoebox or on the shelf in my closet. I just took the money and bought a ticket to visit Marilyn and my mother in Wisconsin.

Granddaughter Hannah ready to kick some butt

TENNIS

I discovered tennis, one of the loves of my life, when the kids and I were living in the Canal area of San Rafael. Tennis was the growing craze in the 70's. My neighbor upstairs and I were looking for another interest to pursue, (not men). We bought a couple of cheap rackets and went to a nearby court. We didn't know at the time that it was not a tennis court, that it was way too small. Somebody came out of the building to inform us.

My only other experience with tennis had been in Wisconsin when I was a kid. A few times a year we would go out into the street and hit tennis balls with old wood rackets. Because there were no fences or nets or lines, it was not much fun. We had to keep chasing the ball before it rolled into the gutter and disappeared down the drain.

When my friend and I took a few group lessons at Albert's Park, I was hooked, especially after the instructor said I had potential.

One day I talked my friend Tam, (the one who took Memo when I went with Cass to deliver the *Amerigo*), into hitting with me.

We were going to Forest Meadows in San Rafael where there were some old courts. I met her outside the apartment with Memo and his little red bike with no brakes. "Do you have to bring him along," she said. This didn't seem quite fair seeing that her little dog Sunshine seemed to go everywhere with her. Sunshine was already in the back seat, nervously pacing about and yapping. "Yes, he has to come," I said, and threw Memo's bike in the trunk.

We climbed the fence to get in. The courts had no nets. We didn't care. It just made it easier to keep the ball in play, and we were just fooling around anyway. I only started to play seriously and passionately in my forties.

Tennis is the best, the most beautiful, and potentially the least expensive sport of all. You can play it all of your life, either competitively or socially. All you need is a racket, which you can buy at the Salvation Army or at a garage sale for $3, some shoes, and a can of balls. (Or you can find used balls in the grass behind the courts).

You do not need a team, you can hit with a buddy or a stranger, or against the wall. If you have fairly decent stokes another person will come up and say, "Hey, do you want to hit?"

Tennis is like a dance, it's also a game where you use psychology and your smarts, like in chess. The biggest and strongest guys are not necessarily the best.

I've taught many adults and kids to play, and over the years I've made some good money from it. For nine years I was also head coach of the San Rafael girls' team. For the past eight years I have been assistant coach of both the boys' and girls' teams. Every one of my children and grandchildren know how to play tennis. I love teaching it.

In the old days it seemed like everybody played. It was before tennis was "privatized." Eventually a bunch of tennis clubs were built due to the realization that money could be made off the popular sport. Nowadays, the public courts are more and more in disrepair, or have been converted into skateboard parks, or parking lots, or outdoor basketball courts. To get into almost all of the so-called "public" courts you need to buy a key.

Tennis has been the most sustaining, time-consuming, and satisfying passion of my life, although I had to quit for ten years from age sixty-five to seventy-five for two hip replacements, three broken arms, and one broken kneecap. My hips breaking down, however, may be due to heredity and not the result of my tennis addiction. Don't blame tennis for anyone's "tennis elbow" either. It's more due to repetitive motion.

When I started playing tennis again at age seventy-five, I experienced a surge of endorphins and I was immediately hooked again. I realized that it was hopeless to ever try to quit, even though now a mysterious pain in my left hip at times makes every step painful. Maybe I will be playing in a wheelchair, (which I have done on occasion), but I will always play.

A toast to Lupe on her 8th grade graduation

THE BLUE HOUSE

The Blue House was blue as the sky after the wind blows all the pollution away. We lived there for almost eight years. It was the closest thing to a normal home that my children experienced in their growing up years.

A few years before, when Cass and I sat Sharon down to tell her that we were getting divorced, she got right up and said, "No big deal." Then she wanted to know who was going to row her and Lupe ashore to go to school.

I had a hard time finding a place to rent when we moved off the boat. Nobody wanted three kids and a mom who worked at a low-paying job as a waitress and was going on a raft trip, but I finally found the apartment in the Canal where we lived for two and a half years. Then, for a couple of reasons, it was time to get out.

When I saw the ad and went to look at the Blue House, I never thought the landlord would let us in, but he did—no references, no credit, nothing. He was an Italian man with a large family and he was from the "old school." He didn't even ask me to fill out an application.

My sister Patty tried to discourage me. "But you don't have any furniture," she said, "and this house is really big." That didn't bother me. We sat on the wall to wall shag carpet flicking ashes into an abalone ash tray. "I've got the floor," I said, and rolled around on the rug.

The Blue House was situated between Jewell Street and a dead end piece of Belle Avenue. The front yard on Jewell Street was all pebbles, with a hill planted in ivy that sloped up to the street. When lying in my bedroom or in the living room on the rug, I looked out on glistening greenery. There was plenty of privacy.

The living room was immense with a fireplace, and off it was a dining area, so big that I could have held a yoga class in it. Off the kitchen, through sliding glass doors, was a deck that looked down on the driveway and a plot of grass that was our backyard.

Off to the side of the house was a vacant lot with a tangle of blackberry bushes, cacti, small trees, and wildflowers. It was wild, undeveloped, and beautiful. Deer, butterflies, and birds were in abundance. In the summer months I would send the kids outside barefoot in the wet grass to pick blackberries for our breakfast.

Memo was just six years old when we moved in. He could ride his bike or his Big Wheel down our piece of Belle nearly to San Rafael High School. The day we moved in, he went too fast and skidded down the asphalt on his face.

I was sitting in the living room on a couple of pillows with a friend and sipping a glass of wine when he came screaming into the house. We put cold washcloths on his head and washed off his face. He continued to scream and scream and scream, and I was not sure about making this move from the Canal to the Blue House.

There were two bedrooms upstairs. A staircase led down to two more bedrooms, a bathroom with a shower, and the garage. Sharon claimed the downstairs. Lupe slept upstairs in Memo's room for the first year. I was afraid to let her go downstairs and be under Sharon's influence. Sharon was in her early teens and a bit moody and belligerent. She usually only came upstairs for meals.

Furniture was acquired little by little. I found a rough picnic table with a wooden splintery bench for the dining room. We still had big pillows in the living room which I was pretty content with, but everyone said I needed a couch, or maybe two couches, to fill the space under the picture window.

The couch I found advertised in the newspaper turned out to be 15 feet long. It was so long that two people could sleep head to toe on it. The couch had a faded gold and brown leaf pattern and cost $34. Memo made forts out of the cushions and slept under them in his sleeping bag.

Believe it or not, forty-three years later, I'm still sitting on that second-hand couch. At some point someone wanted me to get rid of it and find a nicer couch, but the men from the Salvation Army rejected it when they came to pick it up.

After a year in the Blue House we were given a large model upright TV. It looked nice, but you had to hit it hard on the side to make it work. I put photos on it which made our living room look so middle-class America.

In the Blue House there not only was a stove and refrigerator, there was a portable dishwasher all waiting to be hooked up. You wheeled the portable dishwasher over by the sink and connected the hoses to the faucet. The only trouble was that the dishwasher vibrated and shook violently, meandering about the kitchen floor while making a horrible racket. On the occasions that we used it, everyone thought the dishwasher was possessed.

We had many parties upstairs in the Blue House, but I wasn't always aware of the party scene that was going on downstairs. When I was going to school, commuting to Sonoma State for my bilingual credential, we lived in the Blue House. The day that San Francisco Mayor Masconi was shot, all classes were canceled and I got home early.

When I walked into the downstairs, Sharon and her friends were having a mid-day pot party. I was angry and sent everyone away. I found beer bottles behind the couch. I was not opposed to drinking, I was just opposed to Sharon making trouble and getting us evicted. We had a neighbor whose wife sat in a chair by their kitchen window and watched all the comings and goings of Sharon and her friends.

One time I was going to fly to Wisconsin, but the trip was canceled. Sharon was disturbed when I told her that I wasn't going. Then I found out why. "I'm having a party this weekend" she said. I wondered why she hadn't told me. "It's a surprise party," she said. Then I found out that she had invited over 100 people.

The night of the party I took Memo to a baseball game at Albert's park. When we got home, there was no place to park anywhere near the Blue House. We walked up the street. There was a crowd of young people in the driveway smoking and drinking. Upstairs, the music blared. I said "excuse us" to get by all the people lounging on the steps. When we got to the top, a young woman was sitting on a chair near the door.

"Are you on the list?" she asked me, with her pencil poised over a pad.

"I better be on the list. I live here!" I said.

"It's Sharon's mom," someone said, and they let us in.

During the time we lived in the Blue House the front door became warped and it wouldn't close completely. When I heard reports that everyone in the neighborhood was getting robbed, I took satisfaction in knowing that they probably came in to our house, but walked out again because there was nothing they wanted to steal. Except, there was the gun.

Cass said he put his father's gun, a classic model, in my bedroom closet. When it was missing, he accused me of stealing it. I was paranoid thinking that someone had walked into my bedroom and taken the gun. I was afraid that the thief would be back and use the gun on us. In the meantime, I also had Cass's wrath to deal with.

The gun turned up later at his sister's house. Cass had taken it out of my closet, but he hadn't remembered doing it. I was relieved and I could go back to the story that thieves had found nothing worth taking in our house.

I was always scrambling to scrape enough money together to pay the rent, a whopping $400 a month. During the time of the Blue House, my income came from part-time work, student loans, under-the-table jobs, financial aid, and child support. I worried that the landlord would raise the rent and we would lose the house.

One day my landlord came by, pulling up in his red pickup with the name of his construction company on the side. I knew he had been studying for his contractor's license. I saw him get out of his truck and start up the stairs. I was worried because he hardly ever bothered us.

I moved the couch to cover up the hole in the drapes that Peter the rabbit had chewed. I hoped my landlord wouldn't notice the molding around the doors and on the deck or the marijuana leaf stenciled on the downstairs window.

But he had a different mission. He sat down and told me that we would have to move, (unless I wanted to buy the house for $45,000). The year was 1982 or 1983. No hurry, but as soon as we found a place, he wanted to remodel the house and sell it. I knew that we would not be able to stay together. Sharon, then twenty years old, and Diego, her cat, would need to find their own place.

Lupe was graduating from high school. She planned to go away to school, and now she would have to go away. There would not be room for her in the apartment I found next to the freeway by the Civic Center. I tried to make it alright for Memo. "We won't be next to the high school, but there's a McDonald's close by," I said. This was before he had stopped eating junk food and sugar.

Peter, because she was in a cage, got to come with Memo and me, even though pets normally weren't allowed. (Guess what happened to the deck there and those drapes).

Diego and I were the last ones left in the Blue House. I tried to wipe the soot off the fireplace. I scoured the tile in the bathroom and vacuumed the rug, slowly vacuuming myself out of the living room with Diego freaking out. I dragged the vacuum down the steps for the last time. I knew the landlord was going to rip up the carpet, but I cleaned and vacuumed out of respect for the Blue House.

Diego ran away and hid, but there was nothing to hide behind— no furniture just like it was when we walked in eight years ago. I picked Diego up and his claws stuck to the carpet. I pulled him loose and put him in a box in the car to take him to Sharon's friend's place. I drove out the driveway. We left our mark on the Blue House and the Blue House left its mark on us.

YEARS OF RAGING HORMONES

In Eureka before I broke my back falling off the horse, I dated Bob, a tall quiet guy who was in the Coast Guard. He was especially nice and he liked me, but I never felt any excitement being around him. My mother and father and younger sisters came out to visit and they met Bob. My mother's comment was, "She'll never marry him, he's too normal."

In the back of my mind I was waiting for an adventurous, romantic, wild man. That turned out to be Cass.

Right after Cass and I were divorced, I had a few short-term relationships, and then I met Wally. He was physically strong, and also sensitive. I met him at a party that was held in the Blue House. The woman from San Francisco who had found me for Santiago's raft, brought Wally along to my party.

Wally was about my age, had a nice smile, good teeth, bright blue eyes, and a scruffy unshaven look that I found appealing. He operated the Sugar Boat that made daily trips from Richmond to the C&H refinery in Crockett. He lived in a real house and was recently divorced. He also owned a small sailboat! *Too, too perfect.*

A few drinks and the raging hormones took over. He was the last to leave that evening. I remember the shag rug being a little scratchy and the floor in front of the fire place a bit hard, but who cared.

The next night I went to his house in Santa Venetia, close to where the road goes out of town on its way to China Camp. It was a ranch-style house. The sliding glass door of the living room opened onto a backyard and the shallow part of the bay. The waters were lapping right there. Then I saw a big rangy animal bounding toward me. (My granddaughters have accused me of not liking dogs, but that's not true. I just like wild animals better). I quickly closed the door.

Wally definitely had some Cass-like characteristics. He had a sailboat, an outdoor job on the water, and was physically fit. Was I looking for a younger and less controlling version of Cass? Yes, probably so.

A few nights later Wally and I walked down the road to China Camp. It felt so good being outdoors with him in the night air under the stars. We walked holding hands and Wally talked. He told me about his former wife and his kids and several times he broke down and cried. I was a bit surprised.

Wally liked to cook, which I was grateful for, and he liked Lupe and Memo, and they liked him, and his TV. I brought their bikes to Wally's so they could ride around the neighborhood.

The sex was excellent, except sometimes Wally would start crying and talking about past memories, and the good and bad times with his former wife and kids. I thought I wanted a man who was sensitive and emotional, but I wasn't sure how sensitive. I wanted to say, *buck up and get over it!*

One day Wally took me out on his sailboat. Wally's boat was little and unimpressive in comparison to the classic beauty of the *Yo Ho Ho.*

But Wally was good to me. When I was a student teacher in the bilingual credential program, Wally took me out to dinner to nice restaurants. My friend Tam liked Wally. "He says you are hot sex," she said. I don't know how long Wally and I were together, maybe about a year and a half. He mentioned marriage. I had to think about it.

One day I was standing in his living room imagining what it would be like to move into Wally's house and be married to him. I panicked. To be trapped in a house with domestic chores, feeding the dog, and cooking, with a husband who came home from work the same time every night and got up in the morning to go to work. I knew I didn't want that.

One weekend my friend Tam invited Wally and me to go to Ft. Bragg where her boyfriend lived. We would take hikes, go to the beach, walk through the Pigmy forest, and we could play tennis since there were courts nearby. Wally told me that he played tennis.

My feelings for Wally were already cooling off, but I hadn't said anything. On the drive up I felt my mood beginning to blacken. The walks were fine, but when we played tennis Wally was trying too hard and he was terrible. He looked silly to me. We rode home, the two of us mostly in silence, although Tam chatted away.

A few days later he invited the kids and me for dinner. We were supposed to spend the night. I might have unintentionally forgotten. I was down at the high school playing tennis with Frank, Betty, and old Ernie when suddenly Wally appeared at the top of the hill and started screaming, "Where were you? What are you doing playing tennis?"

He caught his breath and yelled some more. "You can just come and get your kid's bikes out of my garage and your clothes out of my house." That was the not-so-pleasant end of our relationship.

Need I mention more? Well, there was a man in Mexico, actually two men. A short story I wrote about one of them is in the back of the book entitled "Merkaba Man".

How do people get through the dangerous years of the raging hormones? Some like me, are lucky. Others are raped, pregnant, suicidal, or killed, or they kill someone. The animal in us seems to run the show.

One day about twenty years ago, I ran into Wally in the United Market. He looked happy and he was smiling. He told me that he was married. After we parted, I was thinking how lucky it was for both of us that we broke up.

TWO FOSTER KIDS

When we lived in the Blue House I had two foster children. The first one was Nathan. He had a cute impish face and it was hard not to fall in love with him. At four or five years of age he was full of energy. It was dangerous to take him into a store. He would grab at anything in sight.

Nathan's mother and brother lived on a houseboat in Sausalito. The little brother was a baby and Nathan's mother could not handle both Nathan and the baby. She took her frustrations out on Nathan, and that's why he ended up in foster care.

I didn't know what I was going to do with him during the day, but thankfully the San Rafael High pool was open to the public in the summer. Nathan didn't know any strokes, but he was completely comfortable underwater. Down he would go and then pop up at some other location in the pool like the little harbor seals. Maybe he was imitating the seals that he had seen in Sausalito.

The lifeguards loved him because he was so cute. He entertained them with his antics in the pool and talked to them when he was out of the water. Right after swimming he lay on the hot cement to warm up and dry out and became as brown as the lifeguards.

Nathan slept in Memo's room and seemed like part of the family. One time an older neighborhood boy had put gum in Nathan's hair. We were driving home from the store when Nathan pointed out the window. "That's him!" he said.

"Stop the car!" yelled Sharon. She jumped out, ran across the street, and grabbed the kid. She shook him and screamed at him. "Don't you ever put gum in my little brother's hair again or…I'll kill you!" she said.

We were aghast. The boy was scared out of his wits and ran home. Nathan calmly continued to suck on the sucker I'd bought him. He probably felt good that he had an older sister who would stick up for him. Sharon had a sense of justice from the time she was a little girl.

Nathan, a cute little imp

After the summer was over, Nathan went back to live with his mother and his little brother. Now I hear he's married and living in Madison, Wisconsin. He found my daughter Lupe on Facebook. Nathan is a man of about forty with a wife and a daughter. I wonder if his little girl is like Nathan was as a little boy. I hope so.

John was another foster child of ours. He was already a teenager when he came to us. His father lived in a trailer park in Corte Madera and didn't want John around anymore. The county paid for foster care for the children that I took in. This was not the only reason I did it. The Blue House was also big enough for another person, although Memo had to share a bedroom. Memo complained about his smelly socks, but otherwise John was welcomed.

John was tall and thin with a thatch of reddish hair. He stooped over when he walked and had a giggly self-conscious laugh. He was enrolled in San Rafael High and Lupe walked with him to school. She was good to him and he adored her.

John was enrolled in a vocational cooking class. One evening we all went to eat at the restaurant where the students prepared and served the food. John was proud to introduce us as his family and the food was excellent.

John was doing all right, but I was going to be commuting to Sonoma State for my bilingual credential so I didn't feel that I could take care of him anymore. I told the social worker I couldn't keep John, and also that I didn't want any more foster children because I was going back to school. John took it very hard.

I think we all knew that John was gay. After he left, he went to live with some older gay men. Then one day I saw in the *Independent Journal* that John was undergoing tests for a new drug for AIDS. A photo showed him bare-chested and thin with a doctor checking him out.

Then a few years later I read John's obituary. He had committed suicide by jumping off the Golden Gate Bridge.

PETER

In the Blue House we also had Peter, who was with us for eight years. Peter was Memo's black rabbit. When Memo was in second grade his teacher kept a rabbit named Leonard in the classroom. When Leonard's "wife" had babies the teacher cleverly created a raffle for one of the babies. The kids in the class sold tickets at a dollar each. I bought one ticket from Memo and thought that was the end of it.

Then one day, when I came home from work at Howard Johnson's, I went into the bathroom and there was a little black rabbit hopping around the toilet.

"Oh no! Don't tell me I won the raffle!"

Memo came running. "No, you didn't actually win," he said, "but I thought you must want a rabbit because you bought a ticket." On the way home he had stopped at the house of the woman we called "the Rabbit Lady" and she'd given him a rabbit.

Peter lived with us longer than either of the foster children. Her legacy, (Peter was really a girl), was quite a bit of damage. She chewed all the electrical cords, all the molding in the house and on the deck. She chewed shoes, and drapes, and my mother's purse.

Memo loved Peter. He dressed her up for Easter and Halloween and put a cat harness and leash on her and took her for walks. Peter did not like me that much. When I vacuumed and had to pick Peter up, she growled at me. I had to approach her from the rear and grab quickly around her plump body in order not to be thumped or bitten.

When we moved out of the Blue House to the apartment next to the freeway in Terra Linda, Peter came with us. The manager allowed us to have a rabbit because it would be in a cage. What he didn't know was that Peter spent most of the time out of her cage, and being a rodent, needed to keep sharpening her teeth.

Memo was away sailing with Cass on the *Wanderbird* when Peter died. Lupe and I buried Peter in Val and Mark's backyard and waited until Memo got home before we told him. Memo was fourteen at the time and the news of Peter's death did not seem to affect him much.

A few months later we moved out and I lost my deposit because Peter had chewed a huge hole in the living room drapes.

Memo's Easter Bunny

When I was at coleman school we had a ribbit in our class. One day his wife hadababie so we had a raffle for the babie, I did not when. when I was walking home I new this laidy that had ribbits. I thought that I could surprise Mary with a ribbit, and new that she would like a ribbit so I got her one. when she got home and she saw the ribbit she said did we when it I said no! I got her from the ribbit laidy Mary screamed that night we cept her in a box. she did not like that the next day we war trying to find a name for her I thought of snoopy that wasddum name

then Lupe thought of Peter I said ok and that is how I have Peter in my

house

"Peter" by Memo Gidley

RELIGION

Because my Irish father was raised Catholic and my Norwegian mother and her family were all Lutherans, as kids we never were baptized and we never went to church. Every time there would be a form to fill out and a question and a blank for religion my mother would write "none." That answer made me yearn for some religious identity. "None" meant you were a pagan, a heathen! You would automatically go to Hell.

When I was young a salesman came door to door with a set of *Uncle Arthur's Bedtime Stories*. My mother bought the series. The books arrived at intervals, full of uplifting stories about good children, prayers, and Jesus.

Somehow as heathens my sisters and I made it through childhood. Then the most extraordinary thing happened. Suddenly we were becoming Catholics. My parents had resolved their religious differences. I guess the reason we got religion was that my Uncle John had died suddenly at age fifty-four. There was a Catholic Mass and burial. My mother and father must have discussed it, but not with any of us girls. My mother was able to convert to Catholicism at that time because her strictly Lutheran father had died, and my grandmother was senile.

My younger sisters were in a normal kid's catechism class to catch up with their peers, but Marilyn and I were too old for that approach.

The two of us were instructed by a Sister Etienne, a pudgy-faced young woman, with skin so white and smooth that I was in awe. Her face lent to caricature. I doodled and drew pictures of her. I was about fourteen at the time and Marilyn was sixteen. One Sunday we were both baptized and confirmed.

After that we had to dress up and go to church—unable to sleep in, or lie around, or have fun outside. At first the rituals, the Latin Mass, the missals that we had, the rosary beads, the singing soaring from the balcony above, and the sonorous voice of Monsignor McDonald stirred my soul. Eventually though the romance wore off.

When Marilyn got her driver's license we didn't go to Mass with the rest of the family. We slept in, then we got dressed up, grabbed our missals, and drove off for an eleven o'clock or noon Mass. But instead of heading to Queen of Peace Church, Marilyn took a different turn and we'd end up at Vilas Park.

We'd take off our hats or headscarves, (required by the church for females), turn the radio on, take out the novel we were reading, kick off our tight shoes, put our feet on the dashboard, and light up a cigarette. After an hour, all refreshed and cleansed from our outing, we would return home for the big Sunday dinner that my mother always cooked.

After my father died in 1961 at age fifty-nine, my mother stopped going to the church, although she continued faithfully paying dues and assessments. Later on a priest would officiate at my mother's service and also at my sister Marilyn's, so I guess it was worth it. All three are buried in the same Catholic cemetery in Madison.

✧

Cass had no interest in religion or church-going. The people Cass knew were rough and tumble fishermen or people who could care less about religion. Cass had no Bible knowledge and I had very little.

One time Cass and I were invited to the world premiere of *The Ten Commandments*. Froggy was about four years old. There was a red carpet leading to the theater. It was a movie in color and a treat for us. We sat enthralled until Abraham took his son up the mountain to sacrifice him for God with a huge knife. Both Cass and I covered Froggy's eyes, not knowing that it was only a test and that God would intervene and Isaac, (or was it Abraham), wouldn't have to kill his son. Thank God for that.

Another scene in the movie depicted Noah's Ark. He got all the animals on board and set off on the ark. There was a huge storm at sea, (which we definitely related to). After the movie let out and we were walking out through the lobby Cass said, "I thought that ark sunk." I tried to hush him up. He turned a few heads with that remark.

✧

I wasn't done with religion just yet. A few years ago my friend Loretta was looking for a place for us to sing. I thought I had a good voice until one time singing Christmas carols in Lake Arrowhead one of the guests turned to me and said, "Better not give up your day job."

After some research, Loretta called me. "We can check out the choir at St. Raphael's tonight," she said. "No obligation, just go and listen." I had my doubts, but said OK.

The director did not waste any time finding music for us and binders. He expected us to join the choir. He asked about our experience and I told him that I hadn't sung in any group since fifth grade. I thought he might let me off the hook, but he was fine with it.

Suddenly I was back inside a Catholic Church. The first Sunday I did not sit with the choir, much too unsure of myself. I had no idea of the structure of the Mass, or when the choir got up and sang. I noticed that before everyone else had received Communion, the choir members put their binders down and filed up to the priest's helpers where they would bow their heads, take the wafer, put it in their mouths and then go back to their seats with hands folded.

Oh shit. I remembered that you were not supposed to take Communion unless you had been to Confession, and it had been fifty years since I had done that. I also knew that it was a Mortal Sin! Loretta was very casual about it, and amused at my reaction. For several Sundays, when she went to take Communion with the rest of the choir, I just stepped to the side and let the other choir members go by.

Eventually I thought I needed to bite the bullet and just go to Confession. I asked my Latina friend, Miriam, to go with me. She was ecstatic to hear that I was going to church. "I have been praying for you to get back in the faith," she said, handing me a rosary.

Since the 1950's major changes had occurred in Catholicism. Confession was not called that anymore. The new term for it was "Reconciliation." There were two priests on duty, one on either side of the church in what looked like closets. People would enter and after a while come out and go kneel in a pew to say their penance.

Miriam went into one box, and then, with great trepidation, I went into the other one. The priest, secluded behind a screen, spoke with a heavy accent. I said the words, "Bless me Father for I have sinned...it has been fifty years since my last confession..." Fortunately he thought I said "fifteen" which was just as well. He wanted to know why it had been "fifteen years." I tried to explain, "Well, you know we lived on a boat..." He still didn't seem to get it. "It just wasn't part of our lifestyle," I said.

It was so stuffy and dark in there that I was sweating. When he let me out, I felt relieved. I only had to say a few "Hail Mary's" and some "Our Father's." Miriam finally emerged. The priest she had confessed to spoke perfect English. He might have asked me many more questions if I'd gone to him. I had been lucky.

After I started singing in the church, my voice got stronger and my range better. I practiced at home and in my car. People noticed. They complimented me on what a good voice I had. I remember driving by St. Raphael's one day and telling myself, *that's my church!* Wow, that felt good and a little strange. I flipped back to the *Uncle Arthur* stories and the days when I wanted not to be a pagan.

However, once again the romance with religion faded and going to Mass got tedious. I used to wear earplugs so I didn't have to hear the homily of one priest. When I fell and broke the bone on the outside of my hip replacement I couldn't go to church to sing. And then Memo had his racing accident. I didn't go back until two years later after Loretta and I went to Mass on one Christmas.

I talked to some members of the choir afterwards. Now I sing, but I don't go to Confession, but I do go to Communion, so I may go to hell. Who knows, maybe when I get to the end of my life, I'll feel compelled to stuff myself into that sweaty little box again and confess a lifetime of sins—just in case.

MY REAL EDUCATION

I've always loved learning, but in high school I did not like chemistry. It was too messy. Measuring things, following a recipe or formula, and washing out containers was like being in the kitchen and cooking, which I also never liked. History was another of my least favorite subjects. It was boring to read about bald old white men and memorize dates and battles. At the University of Wisconsin, European History and Economics were also boring. The material was all so cut and dried and one-sided.

My real education took place a few years later at Sonoma State when I was in the Bi-lingual Education program. It was refreshing to hear another side to the Mexican-American War and to learn about U.S. imperialism and interference in Latin America, South America, the Philippines, Hawaiian Islands, and in many other countries. I realized that my schooling up until then had been more like brainwashing. I had been indoctrinated into this country's beliefs, which included a message of cultural, political, and economic superiority.

Another experience that contributed to my real education was a video course in cultural anthropology at College of Marin. One particularly riveting tape showed a Polynesian culture of so-called "primitive" people living simply and well, eating yams as their major food source. They lived near a river and were happy, healthy, productive looking people, without any technology.

In the video tapes the women were making beautiful baskets and the men were carving and decorating spears for a yearly ceremony. The men would be going out to capture a person from the nearby opposing tribe. Then they would eat the captive. Their culture included cannibalism.

Cannibalism! I was shocked. I shut the tape off just as they were preparing to go out on their mission. I was afraid to look. (My culture uses drones, bombs, and warfare to kill thousands of people, but we don't *eat* them).

Finally, several days later, I got up the courage to watch the end of the tape. I was in for another shock. The men of the tribe were dressed in torn undershirts and dirty shorts. They were sitting on the steps of their huts drinking beer and Pepsi and smoking cigarettes. These formerly proud people looked listless, weak, and sickly. The explanation was that the tribe had been exposed to civilization.

The most mind-blowing and important book that I've ever read is *Ishmael* by Daniel Quinn. In it, the author studies and contrasts so-called "primitive" and "civilized" societies. His quest was to find out "why things are the way they are." He wrote the book in the 1990's as a novel in order to get it published. The main character is a gorilla named Ishmael who educates a man who answered an ad looking for someone who "desires to save the world."

The gorilla speaks of how much "mother culture" determines our attitudes and behavior. We don't realize that the culture we are born into is speaking to us all the time. Mother culture is also telling us that our way is the *right way* to live.

The gorilla points out that traditional societies of man existed for at least a million years living in harmony with the planet. The story that these traditional people operated under was that man is part of the living community, just as all plants and animals. These societies he calls "The Leavers." The premise of the Leavers is that "man belongs to the world."

Then, about 10,000 years ago, came the beginnings of an agricultural society. It operated under a different premise. In the so-called "civilized" societies, humans enact a story in which the planet and all its creatures exist for man's use. The gorilla calls these people the "Takers." The premise of the Takers is that "the world belongs to man." He can do what he wishes with it.

Religion also played a part in promoting the idea that man is the end product of creation and superior to other forms of life. In reality, evolution is what has been and still is taking place.

In the final pages of *Ishmael* the gorilla is dying. His pupil wonders if there really is anything he can do to save the world. Ishmael says that the man will need to teach what he taught him to 100 other people, and those have to teach 100 people more, and on and on.

In the final pages of the book, the gorilla says humans must change the way they think about the world and man's destiny in it if they are to survive. And they must be inventive or there is no hope.

Once you read *Ishmael* you will never see things the same, never think the same, and never behave the same either...hopefully!

"You can't get a man with a gun!"

WORK HISTORY, COLLEGE OF MARIN

After the raft trip I went back to working at Howard Johnson's, but the idea, *go back to school again,* popped into my head. This time I was thinking of bilingual education due to the large numbers of Spanish-speakers who were coming across the border.

I had found my Spanish lacking both in Mexico and on the raft, but it was good enough to get me accepted into the bilingual program. I took out a student loan, cut back my hours at Ho Jo's, and commuted to Sonoma State for the next year. We were living in the Blue House at the time. I ended up with two credentials—one a lifetime Elementary Credential and the other, a Bilingual Cross-Cultural Credential.

It was different when I was actually teaching. There were bells ringing and alarms sounding, money to collect, permission slips, rules, and lesson plans. Plus, teaching took place indoors—no fresh air and no place to run around. Not good for the kids or for me due to me being a push-over, a non-disciplinarian, and an outdoor person. Teaching was not the free and organic learning that I had envisioned. And I was not the one in charge.

After receiving my bilingual credential, I was hired three times by different schools, but I quit or was let go after the first harrowing week. I tried being a substitute but that was just as bad. When the phone rang at 6:30 a.m., it got so I would pull the covers over my head and call out to the kids, "Don't pick up the phone. Whatever you do, don't answer it!"

However, I still thought of teaching as something I could do, just not in a traditional classroom. Lo and behold, I found a more mellow teaching position a few years later at College of Marin.

My friend Lori and I had signed up to take trigonometry in the Math Lab. I was talked into learning higher level math by her because we could share a book and do homework together. Eventually she dropped out of the class and left me the book.

I became friends with the Math Lab assistant named Nadine and I asked about her job. She said that she called the roll and walked around helping students. That was pretty much it. The lab was only open from 10 a.m. to 2 p.m. She got benefits and she could take classes herself.

"That sounds too good to be true. Let me know if you ever decide to quit this job," I said. About two years later, she called me up and said they were looking for someone to take her place. I was coaching the girls' tennis team at the time, so I said no. Also my kids were still young. I had lots of reasons, but the big one was, ugh, *a real job where I would have to report five days a week, indoors?*

The next day the head of the department called me. It was urgent. He needed to hire someone before he left on his boat for Hawaii. In the fall he would be on sabbatical. I hesitated. He said, "You can quit after summer school if you don't like it." So I went in for an interview the next day.

It turned out that the man they had originally hired for the job had decided not to do it, so now I was a shoe-in and the only one they were interviewing. The question they asked me was to explain why "1/a + 1/b does not equal 2/ab". (This is a common denominator problem about the third grade level).

I was to start the following Monday. The morning came. I got in my car. It was about a ten-minute drive to College of Marin, but I remember how time stood still. I felt like I was going to an execution. At every intersection I told myself, *you can still turn around, you can still say no and not show up,* but I kept going.

During the first month I was there I went to a retirement meeting. I got plenty of stares. "What are you doing here? You just started!" said the person sitting next to me. I thought that I could retire after seven years and still get benefits. But seeing that I was only three-quarters time I would have to put in ten. *Ay Chihuahua!*

In the fall, a Mr. Broomis became the new head of the Math Lab. He was so eager to do everything right that he did practically everything himself. He didn't trust anyone to do what he could do, so my duties were less and less. It was a pretty easy job. His manual of instructions to the students became thicker and thicker as he tried to have a rule for every possible loophole and misunderstanding.

Mark Clary, a close friend and part of our extended family, asked me how the job was going. "It's ok, but I don't like the hours. I have to work from 10 to 2 every day," I said.

"What's wrong with that?" he wanted to know. (Mark got up at 4 a.m. every day to work in South San Francisco and didn't get home until 7:30 p.m.).

"Well, it cuts the heart right out of the middle of the day," I said. Mark couldn't get over me saying that.

Just before the ten years were up, I went to the Social Security office to see how much Social Security I could get. The woman gave me some great news. Because we had been married for over ten years and Cass' first wife had died, I was entitled to Cass's social security— a healthy $1,200 a month versus my own benefit which would have been a paltry $471 a month.

I couldn't get both his and my Social Security, but $1200 a month, plus a bit more from PERS, (Public Employees Retirement System), and I would have enough to retire on. I drove home, elated at the good news. *I'm out of there!* A few days later I turned in my resignation.

✧

The day before my final day at the Math Lab was Halloween, and I was in the mood to celebrate. The staff was encouraged to wear costumes. I dressed up as a cowgirl. I wore a blonde wig, a swirling red skirt and fringed vest, and had a black cowboy hat set jauntily on my head. During work hours, I went to several different locations in the building where I danced and belted out, "Oh, You Can't Get a Man With a Gun" and "Doin' What Comes Naturally" from the musical *Annie Get Your Gun.*

Most people didn't recognize me. Not only was I dressed up in a skirt, they didn't relate to my alter-ego self. The bold vivacious woman that surfaced was like a genie popping out of a bottle in front of their faces.

Much as I complained about the Math Lab job that was "eating the heart right out of the middle of my day," the last day was a sad one. I slowly cleaned out my office. When I walked out the door with a few boxes of personal stuff in my arms, I had to say goodbye to my friends, my co-workers, and the tutors and students that had been part of my life for ten years.

At age sixty-one I was suddenly retired. When I drove around doing errands when I ordinarily would have been working, I noticed that most of the people were gray-haired seniors—old souls adrift and unshackled by work in a capitalistic society. I did not feel good identifying with them.

My mental and emotional state took a nosedive for a few weeks. Without a "real" job I had no anchor. I snapped out of it though, partially with the help of tennis. I realized that I could play tennis matches during the day and joined some teams. Also, I could make extra money with private tutoring jobs.

At this time, 2019, I have been retired for twenty-one years. My PERS and Social Security checks keep coming every month. I must admit, the system has worked out pretty good for me.

Me and Marilyn

MY SISTERS

In our family of five girls there were two generations. Marilyn and me, the two oldest, were separated by one and a half years. Then came Phyllis, two years later. We three made up the older generation. There was a gap of six years before Patty was born and two years between her and Carol Mae (Mickey) the youngest. Patty and Mickey were the second generation. It was when my mother was pregnant with Patty that I said, "You get another kid in this house and I'm leaving."

All this time my father desperately wanted a boy. I was supposed to be Marty, Phyllis-Phillip, Patty-Patrick, and Mickey-Michael. And then he gave up, luckily for my mother. When she was pregnant with Mickey, my mother was in her mid-thirties and in late pregnancy became very big and uncomfortable. It was August and hot and humid and she complained about it. She rolled her long nylon stockings down to her ankles and sat fanning herself.

Growing up, Marilyn and I always shared a bedroom. We were soulmates with similar temperaments and the same dark sense of humor, and we were proud of being half Irish. Marilyn used to build me up, telling her friends how talented and smart I was, but she never acknowledged her own talents and worth. When she was feeling down she told me my role was "to fluff her up like a pillow."

Marilyn's the one who wouldn't cry when my mother whacked us with a yardstick and the one who got sent to the closet in fourth grade after she accused the teacher of sneaking the graham crackers that the kids had brought for snack. Marilyn was stubborn and stood by what was right.

Under Marilyn's picture in the yearbook was written "Patience is Powerful." She didn't like the caption and neither one of us could figure out why it was written about her.

Phyllis (aka Fuffa or Fuff) was two years younger than me and I used to give her a bad time. She was fat and I called her "Gibbie" for the Rock of Gibraltar. She would come at me with her fists flying, and I would laughingly hold her off. Phyllis was technically part of the older generation of us Gartland girls, but she had younger friends and ran around with different kids.

Marilyn and I had what we called "best pals." My best pal was Patty and Marilyn's was Mickey. We buttered them up to do our bidding, like fetching our books, getting us snacks, and relaying our messages. They were happy about being our little servants, I mean "best pals."

When we lived on South Shore Drive, Marilyn and I had twin beds in the room overlooking the lake. Phyllis, Patty and Mickey shared a small bedroom. Phyllis slept in the lower bunk of the bunk bed with either Patty or Mickey on top. The other slept in the narrow single bed. There was not much room to walk around.

Under her bed Phyllis kept the supplies to make her favorite comfort food—a sandwich of peanut butter with crushed potato chips on top. Phyllis had the physique of a Sumo wrestler, but this all ended when she was about to go into high school. She suddenly stopped eating and lost weight quickly and dramatically. By the start of ninth grade she had a cute haircut and a perfectly slim body.

About the only trouble Fuffa ever got into was when she was sixteen and had borrowed the station wagon. Marilyn and I sprang out of our bedroom and went to the top of the stairs to listen in to the conversation between two policemen and my parents in the living room. It seemed that Phyllis had driven some girlfriends to the Shuffle Inn. Driving away she had knocked over a garbage pail.

I remember Marilyn and I discussing the incident later and feeling a smug satisfaction that Phyllis had gotten into trouble and had done something to taint her lily-white reputation. Marilyn and I always had the feeling that we were the "black sheep" of the family.

✧

After college, while I was working on a newspaper in Eureka, Marilyn came to live with me. She got a job as a social worker. We lived in an old house that had overstuffed furniture and heavy purple drapes in the living room. It was dark and creepy and we called it the "funeral parlor."

One day Marilyn told me that she was pregnant. It was a "date rape" situation. Unfortunately, in those days any pregnancy was the girl's fault. When my parents came out for a visit that summer Marilyn told them she was pregnant. They took her back to Wisconsin and put her in a Catholic Home for Unwed Mothers in Milwaukee. Marilyn said that my mother never went once to visit her—only my father came to see her.

Marilyn had to give the baby up for adoption. That was the plan and she suffered for it. Marilyn eventually moved to Alaska, where she met her husband, Frank, and was married. They moved to San Diego where they had two children, then they moved back to Wisconsin. After what happened to her, Marilyn was not able to cope well with life. Alcohol was part of her problem. She and her husband divorced. My mother took over much of the raising of the kids.

Marilyn also had physical problems. She underwent triple bypass surgery in her forties for heart problems, and then she developed melanoma in one eye. The eye was removed, but a few years later the cancer spread to other parts of her body. I went to Wisconsin to be with her when she was dying, but she was already in a coma when

I arrived. Marilyn died at age fifty-five.

I am writing about Marilyn because we were so close and because she is not able to write her own memoir. I will also write about Fuffa, (Phyllis), who was killed in a car accident and died at age fifty-nine. I am not writing much about my children or grandchildren because they will have their own stories to tell (and their own version of events).

Phyllis worked in public relations (PR) for the schools in Los Alamos, New Mexico. After the kids grew up and Calvin retired from the Los Alamos lab, he and Phyllis moved to Santa Fe. Phyllis was working for the Los Alamo lab in PR and commuting to her job from Santa Fe. She only had a short time to go before she would retire.

She was newly a grandmother. Her daughter, Kari, and little granddaughter came to visit from California. They were waiting in her Santa Fe home to make Christmas cookies with her. On her way Phyllis' car was hit by a teenager in a huge pickup truck who came across the road and hit her head-on. He had fallen asleep at the wheel. Her side of the car was pulverized. She could only be identified through her wedding ring.

Now, instead of five Gartland girls, we were three. When my mother died, Patty and I had a falling out with Mickey. I won't go into it. After I finish this memoir, I'll see about getting together again.

One hot summer day, a few years after Phyllis died, we held a ceremony to dedicate a bench in Marilyn's and Phyllis' memory. Friends and relatives gathered by the lakeshore under the shade of the huge oak tree.

Earlier in the day my job was picking up trash in the area around the shore and on the rocks by the water. I put on my bathing suit and old tennis shoes and started working. A little old Asian woman who was walking by started to help. I wanted to let her know what I was doing, but she didn't speak any English. It didn't seem to matter. She just smiled and went on picking the garbage up. When we finished we shook hands, and she continued on her walk. I went back in the house all sweaty and grimy to take a shower and get dressed.

During the ceremony I spoke about Marilyn, how much courage she had, and how much I loved her. Kathleen sat on the ground rocking back and forth at her husband Jeff's side. We all knew that Marilyn had a troubled life and her children did not have the happiest time growing up. Calvin and Phyllis' children talked about her. When everybody had said everything, Calvin pulled the cloth off the bench and we all admired it. There were flowers planted by each of the wrought iron legs.

The inscription on the bench gave their names—Marilyn Gartland Keller 1935-1991 and Phyllis Gartland Martell 1939-1997 and then a quote that reads, "Where am I going? I don't quite know. What does it matter where people go? Down to the lake where soft winds blow. Anywhere, anywhere. I don't know..."

I can't remember where I found the quote, and I confess that we tweaked the words to make it say "lake" instead of "river."

After the ceremony everyone went back into the house to eat and to socialize. As soon as I could break away, I ran upstairs and changed back into my bathing suit and went out the door to jump in the lake. I needed to cool off from the hot, humid, and emotionally heavy day.

Marilyn, Phyllis, Me, Patty, and Mickey with our mother

145

STANDING UP TO MOTHER

My slightly crazy sister, Mickey, and her husband, Sheldon, bought a big power boat. It was aptly named *Wild Thing*, which was how Mickey wanted people to think of her. The boat was kept at the pier in front of their house on South Shore Drive. Mickey had cajoled Sheldon, her bookish, intellectual second husband to relocate from Los Angles to Madison in order to be close to my aging mother. Mickey said she wanted my mother to be able to live in her own home as long as possible.

Her idea also included resettling Sheldon's elderly mother there. As a person studying Buddhism, Mickey said she wanted not just to think like the Buddha, but to actually carry out and do what the Buddha teaches.

One day when I was visiting in the heat of summer, Mickey and Sheldon went on a short vacation. They offered the use of the boat to Gary, my niece's boyfriend. Gary jumped at the idea because he liked to fish and now he and I could take the boat out of Monona Bay, under the railroad trestle, and into the big lake. I packed a lunch as we prepared to speed off in *Wild Thing*. My mother was negative about us taking the boat out. She fretted about what could go wrong.

We were having a good time, despite not catching any fish. Then it was time to go home. On the way, our giant horsepower engine began to sputter and cough, and then stop. Gary tried to start it again with no luck. Our solution then was to let it rest. When other boats saw us bobbing around, Gary wanted to pretend that everything was okay. He had his ego and his pride after all. After a while, the engine roared to life again, but only briefly. We were once again left with no power—at the mercy of the wind and waves.

Gary was getting upset. We started drifting again, but this time I saw that the wind and waves were pushing us closer and closer to the rocky shore. I said, "Hey, we've gotta get out of here or we will drift onto the rocks!" I found a red distress flag on the boat and started waving it. Gary continued to pull the cord to try to get the cranky engine going. Finally another boat came along because they had seen our red flag. To hell with Gary's ego, I knew enough to recognize real danger.

The couple on the boat threw us a line and proceeded to tow us away from the shore and slowly toward home. Gary was not happy. When we arrived at the pier and let go of the tow, he got off the boat in a huff. "It wasn't our fault. We didn't do anything wrong," I said. But his ego had been heavily damaged. He went home and I went into the house.

Sure enough, there sat Mother by the picture window, her lips pursed, taking in the whole scene of us being towed back. I knew she would have a lot of "I told you so's" and would blab to Mickey and Sheldon about the incident.

She started to open her mouth, but I spoke first. "I do not want you to say anything to Mickey and Sheldon. I want you to stay out of it!"

She looked at me in shock. "You just keep quiet!" I said. Her mouth snapped shut.

For once I was telling her what to do. I was the adult and she was the kid. I relished the moment and I relish the memory.

The final result was that the relationship between Mickey and Gary deteriorated. Even though the failure of the engine was not his fault, Gary did not want to have anything more to do with the boat, or Mickey and Sheldon, ever again.

MUSKIE FISHING

My father's fishing was not limited to the fish in the lakes around Madison. Every summer we would go "up north" on vacation for three weeks. Our favorite resort was Hahn's Roost on Big Spider Lake. The nearest town was Hayward, Wisconsin, *The Muskie Capital of the World.*

People always said that "pound for pound the fighting-est fish in the world is the muskellunge." A muskie has a wild vicious look, sharp teeth, and a long and lean body. It only develops a big girth when really old and wily.

There was a big rock on the side of the road with Hahn's Roost painted on it that meant we were almost there. There was plenty to do. We swam in the chilly clear water (dreaming of one day making it to the island), lay on the piers in the sun, and played in the old barn where there was a phonograph and equipment to make vinyl records. We read books while swaying in the hammock, carved pieces of wood, and went to town to shop for souvenirs. While we were there my father, of course, had to be indulged in his fishing.

The couple that owned Hahn's Roost kept the grass neatly-trimmed and served meals in the Lodge for those guests who didn't have a housekeeping cabin like ours. I wonder what kind of vacation going "up north" was for my mother. She continued to cook all our meals and clean up after us, although she also used to go fishing in the evenings with my father.

Besides the dinner bell and breakfast bell at the Lodge, there was a muskie bell. When someone caught a legal-sized muskie (more than 30 inches long) the bell was rung loud and clear, like the Liberty Bell. Everyone in the resort dropped whatever they were doing and streamed forth from their cabins. The proud person who caught the muskie was photographed holding the still shimmering fish on a gaff hook.

In addition to muskies my father fished for large mouth black bass. One of us, usually me, got up early to motor or row out onto the lake with him. Sometimes we made our way through the lily pads onto an arm of Big Spider called Little Spider Lake.

When one of us girls went with my father, we usually took a book along and sat in the bow of the boat reading. My father would remind us to check our bait. We'd pull in the line and pretend to check it. We didn't really want a fish to bite our line. I liked eating fish but catching them? No, not really interested. I did not have the patience.

One time when Daddy and I were fishing and I was rowing him next to the shore, he aimed a little too high when he cast. The line snagged in a tree and when he pulled to jerk it free, the line snapped and his pole went sailing through the air. It hit the water, and disappeared in the depths.

It was his favorite rod. We rowed up alongside the spot where the rod had gone down. "Think you could dive down and get it?" he asked. I looked at the unfathomable depths, but I could not see any rod. It didn't matter. "Yes," I said and slipped off my sweatshirt and jeans.

I jumped off the side of the boat. On the first two attempts I came up gasping for air with no pole. Then, on the third dive down, I felt the rod and wrestled it free. I triumphantly thrust it skyward as I kicked my way to the surface. My father said he saw the rod coming up first. He was ecstatic and very proud of me.

To fish for muskies you need to cast your line out as far as you can and then slowly reel it in to make the lure look as lifelike as possible. The colorfully painted lures had rows of nasty hooks and wiggled as they came through the water.

One afternoon when I had gone muskie fishing with Daddy, I was having fun seeing how far I could cast the line out. Suddenly the rod bent over and was almost jerked out of my hand. Something big was on my line and it wasn't a weed! "Help!"

"It's a muskie!" my father yelled. The fish jumped clear out of the water, did a few twirls, and then flopped back in the water and took off in a direction away from the boat.

Daddy was just as excited as me. "Give him a little slack then reel him in again!" My muskie jumped way out of the water again. I held on, then gave it some more slack. The third time it jumped, it twisted like a bronco in midair and shook the lure loose. My beautiful fish took off, and I was left holding a limp line, with my heart beating like crazy.

Wow, what a thrill! I then realized the kind of high that fishing gave people like my father.

My father also fished for muskies in other lakes in northern Wisconsin with his brother and other men. I'm sure he caught some, but it was my mother who rang the muskie bell one evening at Hahn's Roost. She is faintly smiling in the photograph.

After we grew up there were many years and decades of not going "up north." Then one year when I was in my fifties, my sister decided we all needed to make a pilgrimage back to Hahn's Roost.

We reserved two cabins. One was "Balsam Hill" which was the cabin we always stayed in. The years had taken their toll. The ceilings sagged and the floor sloped, and my father was no longer alive. My grandson Riley was about two years old. I remember my mother saying she didn't want him to eat in her car, and him staring back at her with a fistful of crackers.

My niece and I swam to the island that we could never reach as kids. It wasn't that far from the shore, but the water was very cold, and I was hypothermic by the time we got back. My son-in-law rented two jet skis that we raced around on the lake.

Because we didn't do any fishing, and without my father there, Hahn's Roost was not the same.

DADDY 2

Much as I railed against my mother and thought I loved my father a psychologist once said, "It's not your mother you have a problem with, it's your father." Why did she think that? I remember mostly the daddy that I loved. Our neighbor told me how lucky I was to have him as a father, but now I remember a dark side that she didn't know about.

There was not a lot of tenderness between my mother and father. I never saw them kiss each other, hug, or hold hands. It was as though by the time I was a little girl any love they had for each other was over. My mother was brought up by stern Norwegian parents. I'm sure her feelings were stifled. My father was one of four boys and had two older half siblings. He was the youngest, the one who probably got away with everything.

My father was a witty, fun-loving man. He also had a sharp tongue and loved to tease. He would upset my grandfather, making him angry when they talked politics. He made fun of my mother. He pushed my buttons, making racial insults or jokes just to needle me. My father often called my mother the "Old Battle Axe." Sometimes we would be eating in the kitchen and he would say something critical or cutting. She never tried to fight back. She'd just start crying, get up, and leave the table.

Although he had a great sense of humor, my father was extremely absent-minded. One time around the holidays he was driving us somewhere and he went through a red light. We almost got hit by another car. He said later that he thought the red and green stoplights were Christmas lights, that's why he drove right through the intersection.

Another bad thing about my father was that he smoked. The downstairs bathroom was tiny with just a toilet and sink. We complained every morning about the smell after he was in there smoking and going to the bathroom. When he got older and wasn't feeling well, he went for treatments to the chiropractor who lived across the street. But it was his heart that was bad, probably from all of the smoking. He suffered a heart attack one wintry day changing the tire of my sister Phyllis' car.

I flew in from California. We took turns being by his side in the hospital. One night while I was asleep, my mother and sister Marilyn were called in to the hospital. Marilyn, who had worked as a nurses' aide, knew my father had died when she saw his slippers in a paper bag at the foot of his bed. Daddy died in the hospital at age fifty-nine. He was given a Catholic funeral and was buried in the Catholic cemetery.

Once when I visited Madison many years later, Marilyn and I were walking near the zoo in Vilas park. She had been undergoing therapy. She announced that we were sexually abused as children saying "that was what the enemas were all about."

I didn't want to hear it. It made me feel sick. But she was right about the enemas and about her and me having some of the classic symptoms of abuse. She claimed that my mother held us down while daddy "did it to us."

Hmmm, I remember hating the enemas which were given to both of us at the same time, supposedly because we were constipated. I shoved this memory deep in my psyche. Whatever happened to us wasn't good, but I also think the symptoms that we exhibited could have been caused by my mother calling Marilyn and me "lazy good for nothings" or hitting us with the yardstick.

I should have asked my mother about the enemas before she died. Another question I have for her would have been, "Why did you get rid of all the photos of my father right after he died?" I remember there was one photo of my father sitting in a boat with his brother while they were fishing for muskies up north. My father had stuck a pencil or pen under his sweater so that it looked like he had the pointed tits of a pinup girl. He was grinning at the camera as he posed for the photo.

There's another bad daddy memory. I was about thirteen years old. I was angry about something and ran upstairs and slammed the bathroom door. My father ran up the stairs after me. How did the timing work? How could I have already been nude and ready to step into the bathtub by the time he bolted up the stairs and pushed the door open? I screamed when he came in and saw me naked. I felt shame and horror.

A similar scene occurred in a movie preview that I saw recently. Suddenly a man, (he was a stranger), enters a woman's bathroom by mistake. "Did he see? Did he see me?!" She is outraged and mortified just as I was.

So I stopped talking to my father. *How could I talk to him after that?* The silence between us lasted for two years. Nobody in my family said a thing about it. That's how we dealt with emotions and our relationships.

A slobbery kiss from grandson Riley

PLAYFUL GRAMMA

First I was the mother of Sharon, (aka Froggy), Lupe, and Memo. Now I am a grandma, although according to my friends Mark and Val's daughter, Sarah, I shouldn't have been a grandma. Lupe had just come to Marin and had announced that she was pregnant. Little eight-year-old Sarah and I were in my car driving somewhere when she suddenly said, "Mary, I just can't see you as a grandma."

"Why is that?" I asked.

"You're just too active!" she said, shaking her head.

But I became a grandma anyway. First there was Riley, the boy, and then came Hannah, then Rosie, then Cassie, then Ava, then Rachel, then little Sophia. So now there are seven, and I have definitely been "playful," and maybe a little "too active.

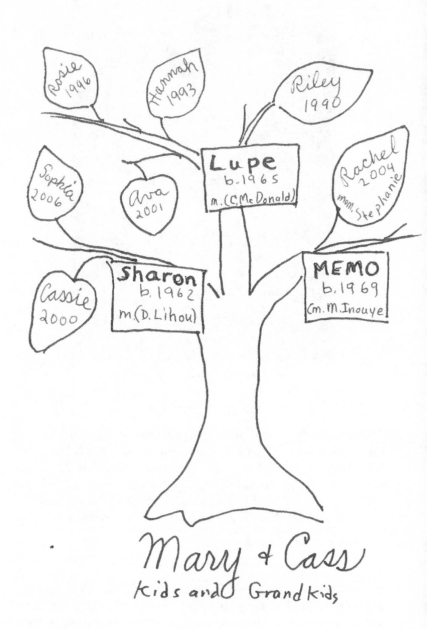

Mary & Cass
Kids and Grandkids

When Riley was five years old and in kindergarten he came home with me from one of Memo's races in Long Beach. Val, Sarah, Riley, and I were all in the car with Val driving. She inserted a tape of Sarah as a toddler talking and singing little songs, very boring when it wasn't your cute kid. She had a stack of these tapes.

I turned to Sarah and Riley and said, "I wonder how many times we can sing '99 Bottles of Beer On the Wall' before we get to San Rafael." Riley, who was the most energetic, exuberant, mischievous, sassy little boy, joined in boisterously as we sang it over and over. Val drove on, but with the tape deck silenced.

When we got home and into my apartment I made Mac and Cheese for dinner. Riley sat down and let out a big "Whew." He grinned at me and patted my arm. "No more mean old mommy," he said, "just a playful gramma!" He looked at me adoringly. Now how Lupe could ever be called a "mean old" anything beats me, but perhaps some of Mister Riley's errant behavior had even gotten to Saint Lupe.

I do love being a gramma, but I had to lay down one or two rules. The first rule was "a playful gramma does not change poopy diapers." Or so I thought.

I got stuck once when I was in Lake Arrowhead. Lupe had left to meet Chris in LA for a night or two. Ava was a big chunky baby at the time with a big appetite. Luckily helpful Hannah was home when Ava emitted a horrible smell in the diaper area.

"Hannah, help me. Help gramma. I need you!" I yelled. It was not always easy to locate someone in that three story giant house in the mountains.

Hannah eventually showed up and said, "Pyewww. Look, it's leaking out of the sides of the diaper!"

"Coo, coo," said Ava, enjoying the fuss being made over her.

We hauled her at arm's length into the room with the changing table and set her down. "Don't you dare move," said Hannah. It took the two of us to pin her down and clean up the poopy diaper mess. I could not have done it alone.

And that's the only diaper that this gramma remembers ever dealing with, but it was a biggie and I deserve a prize. When Ava was a little older she used to try to get someone to wipe her butt when she went poo-poo in the toilet.

I would invariably be sitting quietly at the kitchen table drinking coffee and eating my breakfast. "Diarrhea gramma, di-aaa-reeee-aaa," Ava's voice shrieked from the bathroom.

There are many other grandchildren stories which I call "Life Stories." Before they got too old to enjoy them, the tradition was for whoever was awake first to come into my room with a cup of fresh hot coffee and climb in bed with me for story time. I made up stories improvising as I went along, sometime having to ask for their help. "Give me an animal," I'd say and then after a few gulps of coffee I was off.

After the make-believe stories it became the tradition to tell "Life Stories." I have some about every grandchild, but most are about what Ava did. Second in quantity are stories about Riley. They were two of a kind!

Now my grandchildren are too big and too old to climb in bed with me for stories. That is very sad. The last little one was Pia, who would brave the cold rain in Newport, Oregon to come out to the trailer with a cup of coffee sloshing around in her trembling little hands. After she climbed in the bed we would turn the EB up to Hi and settle back to tell stories. We added stories about the tennis balls that I slept with. There was Ball Girl, and there was Penn and Dunnie (Dunlap).

Now maybe even Pia is too old. I know for sure that the next youngest, Rachel, is too old.

The following are a few of our favorite "Life Stories." I have only included some of the classics.

Riley

One time in La Paz I was taking care of Riley and Hannah so that Lupe and Chris could go to Todos Santos. In the morning I took the kids on a walk on the *malecon*. I was pushing eighteen-month-old Hannah in the stroller when Riley said he wanted to push her. *What a good big brother.* When he got to the top of a very steep handicap ramp, Riley gave the stroller a little push, let go of it and said, "Whee!" Hannah careened down the ramp, crashing at the bottom.

She ended up face down with a mouthful of sand. Grandma was very angry at Riley.

✧

One time when Memo was in the school at Laguna Seca, we went there to see him race. One of the guys at the track asked four-year-old Riley if he wanted to sit in the racecar. Riley did, so the guy lifted him into the car. A moment later Riley looked up and said, "How do you start this sucker?"

Hannah

One day when Lupe was visiting Marin, *Quiz Show*, a movie Chris was in was playing. Hannah was a breast-fed baby, but I told Lupe to go to the movie. She left a bottle of formula just in case and instructions on how to fix it. I was hoping Lupe would be back before Hannah woke up, but the movie was a long one. After a couple of hours, Hannah started making sounds that escalated into loud crying. I hastened to heat the bottle. I put a drop on my arm to test it, but the formula was too hot. I ran it under the cold water, then it was too cold. I finally got it to the right temperature and picked up a screaming Hannah. Lupe didn't think she would take a bottle, but when I held it near her, Hannah snatched the bottle from me and chug-a-lugged the whole damn thing.

✧

When Hannah was old enough, I wanted to take her to the Math Lab. I bragged to all my co-workers what a sweet little girl she was. (Riley had been there many times and had a reputation). "She's so cute and she doesn't make any noise. You are going to love her," I said. On the way to the Math Lab, I stopped off at another office to show Hannah off. The woman there decided that Hannah should have something to play with and gave her a big tub of Legos. To get to the Math Lab we had to walk through the library. Hannah and I were happily on our way when *splat*, Hannah fell. The tubful of Legos landed all over the floor and Hannah howled like a banshee.

Rosie

One day when all of us were in Crescent City, Patty's husband Jon accidentally made Rosie hit her head. She started to cry, and Jon said he was sorry. Through her tears Rosie spat back, "Sorry doesn't count!'

✧

I was visiting at Lupe and Chris' first house in Lake Arrowhead and taking care of the children so that Lupe could go to LA. Lupe told me I could sleep in the master bedroom with Rosie who had recently been weaned. I finally got Riley and Hannah calmed down and into their beds. Then I settled down in the big bed with Rosie. A little while later Rosie sat up in bed and started crying, "I want mama. I want my mama." I tried to comfort her, but it was no use. She only screamed louder for her mama. Then I told her, "Grammie be right back, honey," and I went upstairs and grabbed my earplugs. I slipped back in bed again and patted her on the back. "It's ok, Rosie, Grammie's here," and I went back to sleep.

Ava

When Ava was riding in her car seat and her older siblings were talking, laughing, and carrying on, she would interrupt them by yelling, "Hey everybody, listen up! Hey, listen up, guys!" They would turn around, "What, Ava, what?" She would get a devilish look on her face, and say, "Apple-sauce." They would crack up, and she would think she had just said the funniest thing ever.

✧

Ava gives Harry the hamster to Rosie to hold. Harry pees on her. Rosie screams and drops him on the table, knocking over Gramma's water glass. Ava picks up Harry and says, "It's nothing personal, Rosie. He's peed on me three times." Lupe thinks Gramma is wiping up the pee with the kitchen sponge, but it's just the water from Gramma's glass.

Rachel

At Patty's gym in Crescent City, Rachel has a T-shirt on that reads "I Get My Good Looks from My Mom." The girls at the desk were remarking on it. Then one of them asked Rachel what she gets from her dad. "My Cytomax," she said.

✧

Gramma had the reputation of chewing a bite of food at least fifty times before swallowing. One day Rachel gave Gramma some advice on how to gain weight. "You don't have to eat more," Rachel said, "you just have to chew less."

Cassie

When it was Halloween, Cassie refused to put on the clown costume, no matter how much we pleaded with her. Then Sharon went to work. When night came, the doorbell rang and some kids in costumes appeared at the door. Dave got out a bag of candy and gave a handful to each kid. Cassie wanted to know why, and Dave explained. Suddenly Cassie said, "Hey, where's that clown costume?"

✧

After visiting in Lake Arrowhead, Cassie went back home to Newport. Gramma called her on the phone. "I bet you miss all your cousins, right?" Cassie answered, "No, but I miss Lupe."

Sophia

Sophia said, "I wish I had a dog like Taku." (At the time, Taku was their dog).

✧

Sophia went to visit Gramma and saw all the photos of the kids on the refrigerator. She pointed to the picture of Riley and said, "Who's that?" Gramma told her that it's her cousin, Riley. "Oh yeah, he's my favorite," she said.

Grand kids!
Top: Hannah, Riley, Rosie—Bottom: Cassie, Ava, Rachel, Sophia

MY TUTORING CAREER

My first tutoring job was a work-study position at Sonoma State. I enjoyed working in the tutoring center and getting paid for it. In the tutoring center, the students were not isolated in lonely little desks. They could talk to each other and we could talk to them. I tutored Spanish while I was studying for the bilingual credential, and also tutored English and ESL (English as a Second Language).

After I "flunked out" of teaching, (I was not cut out for a regular classroom), the Sonoma State experience gave me an idea. I could tutor students privately. I didn't have to be in a classroom. I began tutoring on a limited basis, mostly elementary students before I was hired for the Math Lab.

When I started teaching math at College of Marin, I found that it was a subject that the majority of students hated. They would tell me, "I'm just a right-brained person." This always struck me as strange since I knew people had both a right and left brain.

While working in the Math Lab, I taught all levels of arithmetic, algebra, and trigonometry. After I retired it was a natural progression from the Math Lab to the highly lucrative job as a private math, English, and Spanish tutor for high school students.

I lived a half a block away from San Rafael High. Most of the parents paid me in cash, or if they preferred to write a check, I put it in a special checking account.

Typically, the students would come over after school or I would drive to their homes in the evening. My granddaughter Rachel was present for a few tutoring sessions. She drew a picture of me looking very stern and teacher-like. Her drawing was titled *a Pichter of my AweSome grandma.*

One day a student asked to use my phone to call his mom. I directed him to my wall phone in the kitchen. He stood there, helplessly. "Uhh, how do you work it?" I had to show him how to dial a number on an actual dial phone.

Another boy told me that his day had "not been too good." Somebody had stolen his iPod out of his locker. "Ahh too bad," I said, but I had no idea what he was talking about. When his mother came in to pick him up she was upset, and I found out that it was a $150 item.

My best student money-wise was a boy I tutored almost every day of the week for about three years. I helped him in geometry and Spanish and then in advanced algebra, which he needed in order to apply for college. His name was Joseph. He was a very methodical and thorough student. We did every single homework problem together. He bought me a sandwich at Sol Food when he graduated.

His father would drive up in his Mercedes after he'd dropped Joseph off at San Rafael High and call to let me know he was downstairs. I'd run down, sometimes with a coat over my pajamas, and he'd hand an envelope full of cash to me out the window of the car. I'm not sure what people thought who saw this transaction— probably that it was a drug deal.

During my tutoring years the woman at the counseling center at San Rafael High kept my resume on her bulletin board and recommended me before the other tutors. I got so busy that some- times I had to turn students down. For the most part, I loved tutoring the kids on a one-to-one basis. There were only a few that were problems.

There was a boy named Ben who had ADHD to the extreme. He was in the eighth grade and his grandma was his guardian. I could not get him to sit in a chair for even five minutes. I tried setting my oven-timer to three minutes, but he couldn't sit for even that long. He spotted my orange metal basket of tennis balls, leaped up, and began hitting them into the ceiling.

We met about ten times with no success. I found out that his grandma had refused to let him take any medication or to be put in a special class because she wanted him mainstreamed. I felt sorry for his teacher.

My retirement from tutoring came shortly after I flew over the handlebars of my bike and broke my right arm. It happened one afternoon when I had met my friend Charlotte for coffee at Peet's and was riding home to see my students. The gears froze up and I got thrown over the handlebars. A good Samaritan helped me home and wheeled my bike into the garage. I just had time to get the large ice pack out of the freezer before the doorbell rang. It was final exam time and I didn't want to cancel my appointments.

I laid my right arm on the ice pack and wrote left-handed that day. I tutored six students in a row with a broken arm. After the last student left, I drove myself to Emergency at Kaiser Hospital.

When technology came to the high school and all the tutors were asked to post their qualifications online, I didn't do it. I was ready to quit anyway.

A few years ago, I had another job tutoring my granddaughter Rachel in math over the phone. She was in the sixth grade when they sprang Common Core math on the kids and the teachers. The teacher was defensive about not explaining the material to the students. "We are learning this together," she said.

It was not easy tutoring Rachel over the phone, especially since her cell phone had terrible reception. But we did it. Memo and Rachel framed a copy of her grades for me. Rachel also made me a card entitling me to a "free lunch at any restaurant you want." I haven't cashed it in yet.

I also stopped tutoring because I started helping coach the San Rafael girls' and boys' tennis teams. There was no money involved, so maybe it was not smart because I was making $40-$45 an hour when tutoring. However, coaching meant sunshine and tennis, and that was priceless.

PART 4: ENJOYING THE RIDE

WISCONSIN REVISITED

I'm at home in Wisconsin, upstairs scribbling in a notebook. My mother is downstairs vacuuming. I'm sixty-five years old, but it's still "outside" where I want to go—where I feel most alive and most like me. I will try to sneak down through the kitchen and run out the side door. But then the vacuuming stops and a little while later I hear the back door close. She's gone. It's safe for me to go downstairs.

I'm here on a visit, and I've stepped back in time. The house is haunted. All the same things are here as if the ghosts of those gone are still around.

I walk through the living room with its threadbare carpet and old lamps and drapes from 1951. The 1950 World Book Encyclopedias are in the bookcase in the dining room. It's afternoon and the sun strikes me right in the eye when I sit at the head of the table. The chairs around the table always squeaked, and they still do. The huge dieffenbachia, a jungle plant, loves the sun. It has resided in the corner of the room since we moved into this house.

We rarely ate in the dining room, instead we squished all seven of us into the nook in the kitchen. Whoever got there first ended up trapped in back of the table. To escape you had to slide down and crawl out, suffering a few kicks on the way.

I open the door that leads from the kitchen to the basement, and it smells exactly like it did fifty years ago. I walk down the stairs and see my old skis and skates, full of dust, hanging up. There are some air mattresses and a rollaway bed. Did my grandmother sleep on it? No, I remember now that she slept in the enclosed porch. In my father's office are his fishing rods and tackle box. On the old desk, his manual adding machine, some old papers, and a portable file.

I've seen enough and start to leave the basement. I see the chain around the post where my dog was tied and her old water dish. It brings back memories of K.D.

When I was about twelve years old, I wanted a dog—badly. It had to be a Boxer, probably because there was one down the street. They kept him tied on a long lead in their backyard. He was just a puppy with big paws, and he jumped up and slobbered all over me. I thought he was cute with his fat heavy head, big square muzzle, and big brown eyes. I would stop and wrestle with him on my way to school.

I desperately wanted a Boxer, but my father wanted a hunting dog, so we got an English Setter. We drove all the way to Nebraska to get her. They were supposed to be really good bird dogs, but mine was wild and crazy. She was always getting into trouble.

Her name was Nebraska Katrina Lu (K.D. for short). We could never take her off the leash because she would take off like a rocket, but she was great for hitching up to a sled and pulling us across the ice when the lake froze over. When I graduated and moved to California, the dog was left with my mother.

On this trip I am noticing how green Wisconsin is. There are greens of many different shades. What are the names of all those shades of green? Leaf green, grass green, algae green, corn green, weed green? Green is the color of the Wisconsin countryside during the summer.

There are so many things that I love about Wisconsin that we don't have in California. I love the fireflies—magical, spirited, and fleeting. Trying to catch one is like trying to catch a soap bubble. I love the varieties of clouds. One minute there isn't a cloud in the sky, but suddenly they appear like actors on a stage. They are continually moving and always changing shape and size. The sun is patient as the clouds play in front of it.

Suddenly there can be dark clouds, more humidity, and the smell of rain and a storm. The wind comes before the rain. There will be lightning and thunder—the closer together they are, the closer they are to YOU. The flashes of lightning can light up the entire sky or come in jagged rips. Then it's raining in big fat heavy drops. We are running back into the house, running around shutting all the windows to keep the rain out.

Now I go outside and across the street by the lake with its rocky shore and murky green water. The bench, dedicated to my sisters, is a new addition. Coneflowers and purple yarrow are planted on either side.

In my imagination Marilyn and Phyllis are sitting on the bench. What are they saying to each other? The slightly mad one and the practical one. My reverie is interrupted. Mother is calling.

"What are you doing over there? It's time for lunch."

RACHEL AND HER CELL PHONE

I've been known as "Playful Grandma" but the kids are all getting older now and they all have cellphones, and they don't play! I feel antiquated.

Today in the car Rachel hides her cellphone in her lap. She knows I don't want her to be on it when I drive her home to Placerville, but she sneaks it out.

Before the era of her cellphone, when we were in the car she would read the books that I brought from the library, or read from my joke book, or tell me about her life—whether it was about nursery school where her boyfriend wore pull-ups, or her dog that was pregnant, or how spoiled her brother was.

Today we talked a little. She said that she wouldn't want to be home-schooled because home-schooled kids are "socially awkward." This is not the first time I've heard her use that term and I'm sure she would have applied it to me.

Cell phone no. 1 was a smartphone her other grandma gave Rachel when she was just eight years old. I went to pick her up because we were flying to Oregon to see Sharon and Dave and her cousins, Cassie and Pia. Rachel's grandma ran around her house frantically looking for the charger so Rachel could take the cellphone with her. If I had only known the obsession that followed I would have said, "Forget it. Let's leave the phone here."

In Newport we were riding in Sharon's car, and I was in the back seat with the girls. Cassie was twelve years old and had a smartphone. I'm not sure where we were going, but both Cassie and Rachel were busy thumbing away, playing games, communing with the under-world for all I know. Pia had no smart-phone, not even a dumb flip-phone like mine.

When cellphones first appeared and before texting, they annoyed me to no end. On the Airporter, cell phone people had long loud conversations. In the library, in the grocery stores, or as they were crossing the street, cell phone users were engrossed in their phones, oblivious to their surroundings or to other people.

One evening coming home on the Airporter, the woman behind me started setting up appointments with her clients on her cell-phone. I turned around in my seat, and snarled at her to not do her business on the bus. "I don't want to listen to it," I said. She didn't apologize, but she shut up.

The night that Rachel and I were coming home from Newport, it was very late. We took a taxi from the Transit Center to my apartment. When we walked in the door I casually asked Rachel where her cellphone was. She looked in the plastic bag and dumped everything out on the floor.

"It's not here! Grandma my cellphone is gone!" and she started crying hysterically and shaking uncontrollably. "I don't know where it is."

I grabbed her. "Take it easy, calm down now, let's backtrack. Did you have it in the cab?"

"Yes! I put it in this bag, but it's gone! What am I going to do?"

"Well, it's somewhere, maybe it fell out in the cab. What was the name of the cab?"

Neither of us knew, only that it was a black car and the driver was in the front of the line of cabs.

"Let's go back to the Transit Center, the taxi might still be there," I said. We jumped in the car.

We scanned the line of taxis, no black ones, but I went to the taxi driver in the front of the line. He rolled down his window. He knew who the black taxi driver was and had his number. He put in a call. A while later the driver called him back. Yes, he had found Rachel's cellphone on the floor of the backseat, but he was done for the day and he was in Novato. Okay, he would come down.

Rachel and I sat huddled together on a bench at the Transit Center. It was getting close to 11 p.m. We waited a long time in the dark, freezing cold. We were hopeful, but also a little afraid that the black taxi would not come back.

But it finally did return, and the driver handed the cellphone over to Rachel. I think I gave him a few dollars. I can't remember. Rachel and I both slept fine that night, but I doubt if either of us would have slept at all if we hadn't found that damn cellphone.

In my mind it's a crime to give a kid a cellphone. There goes creative play, there goes imagination, there goes reading books and telling jokes, there goes childhood! And adults and their cell phones are just as bad.

MEMORABLE ACCIDENTS AND OPERATIONS

Am I accident prone? I don't think so. But if you live long enough, as I have, the list will be extensive. As far as operations go, I've also had my share.

1945: First operation—I was eight years old and Marilyn, Phyllis, and I all had tonsillectomies at the same time. We were bribed with "you will get to eat all the ice cream you want."
Result—I learned you can't trust what an adult says.

1947: Accident—Broke bone in foot running into second base, which was a fire pit in the vacant lot.
Result—I thought crutches were cool, at first.

1959: Accident—Fell off horse in hills near Eureka and crushed three vertebrae in lower back.
Result—Going stir-crazy went to a bar with brace on back and met Cass.

1963: Operation—Surgery at the Marine Hospital to clean out dead fetus due to "missed abortion".

Result—No longer pregnant. Major traumatic experience. Needed to decide what to do next.

1970: Accident—Fell down open hatch of Cass' fish boat carrying load of dishes to wash on the dock. Three broken ribs.

Result—Feeling sorry for self, started bumming cigarettes from the Mexicans that Cass had smuggled up to work on fish boat.

1989: Operation—Surgery to drill holes in my sinuses to treat nosebleeds and infections.

Result—When Memo asked me to deliver his plate (he was on crutches) I told him I wanted to live alone. He moved out the next day.

1989: Operation—Shoulder surgery, right shoulder (torn muscle and impingement of right shoulder).

Result—After I was sedated, surgeon said he was a tennis player and had the same problem, but he elected not to have the surgery.

1990: Accident—Broke bone of hip in Wisconsin racing Memo and Mickey on ice. Fell as I slid across the finish line.

Result—When I was on crutches, Memo planted the fart machine next to me in the airport and walked away. He pressed the button many times. I had my ear plugs in so I didn't realize why everyone near me got up and walked away.

1990: Accident—Broke big toe at swim meet when teammate dropped heavy table on my foot.

Result—Acquired habit of sleeping with foot in a box. Discovered that bad habits, e.g. sleeping with foot in box, are harder to break than good ones.

2003: Operation—Right hip replacement. I was sixty-six years old. Doctor said, "You're one of the young ones and should be sent home."

Result—Threw up and fainted. He sent me to Smith Ranch Rehabilitation Center.

Result II—Wrote a story about my roommate in rehab center entitled "Home."

Result III—Memo said, "Don't worry, you're never going to have to go to a place like that." (I should have gotten that in writing).

2007: Operation—Left hip replacement. I was seventy years old. No more hips to worry about.

Result—Every time I fly, security is a double nightmare.

2008: Accident—Broke left arm and broke kneecap while riding bike with Lori and gazing at a tree.

Result—Learned not to sight-see while riding bike.

2009: Accident—Broke left arm again- Running in rain from Transit Center, slipped on metal plate, fell face first halfway into the street during five o'clock traffic.

Result—Smashed face and broken arm. Doctor said, "Not you again."

2010: Accident—Third broken arm- As I was leaving Peet's Charlotte said, "Ride carefully." Almost home, the gears locked up, and I went flying over the handlebars. After I finished tutoring six students, I drove myself to Emergency.

Result—Decided not good to say "ride or drive carefully" to anybody.

2014: Accident—Broke bone outside hip replacement. I was stretching after tennis with my leg up on a planter. When I tried to pull my leg down, the heel of my shoe caught and I fell back onto the pavement. My friend Mary Beth took me to Kaiser. I walked in, but went out in a wheelchair. I was told to stay off my right leg for twelve weeks.

Result—Found out who my true friends were.

2014: Accident—Memo's crash. He broke fourteen bones, underwent five or six surgeries, spent several weeks in two different hospitals and then a month in a rehab center. It took four years of slow and painful recovery before Memo was healed and back in a race car.

Result—Every accident and operation of mine seemed in-significant in comparison.

2018: Accident—Tripped and fell over hazardous parking barriers at the high school while coaching tennis. Injured entire right side, with occult fracture of elbow. School's insurance company didn't want to pay. Finally settled out of court.

Result—I am determined to never fall again and to never have another operation.

RACECAR MAMA

When Memo was about two years old, a couple and their little boy came to dinner on the *Yo Ho Ho*. The boy had two little Hot Wheels that he ran up and down the table on the boat going "Vroom vroom." He gave Memo a car to play with. Memo had only seen the dolls of his sisters before then. When it came time for our guests to leave, Memo wouldn't let go of the car. He had a total meltdown.

When Memo was three years old he backed his little pedal car off the dock and went down into the icy waters of San Francisco Bay. Cass fished him and his car out. I thought then he would be cured of cars but not so (although first he was fixated on racing bicycles and motorcycles).

Memo started racing bicycles as a boy, and then motocross as a teenager. At the first motocross race I went to at Sand Hill there were two ambulances standing by. This was not reassuring. The first accident happened in the warmups, before the race even started. There was another accident during the race, and another rider went down. A woman, his mother, went running out onto the track, and kneeled down beside him until the paramedics came. I was thinking that I did not want that role. Memo was bound and determined to race, however, and I was fated to become "Racecar Mama."

While racing motocross, Memo suffered a broken arm when he was in the eighth grade, and then a broken foot when he was still living at home and taking classes at College of Marin. The last fracture was a bad one and required surgery. Afterwards Memo was on crutches.

I was carrying his plate for him when suddenly I'd had enough. I told him I wanted "to live alone." He wanted to know when I was moving out. *Ha Ha.* The next day he bounced his dresser down the stairs and found a place to live with some friends.

Shortly after that, Memo's Uncle Jon took him to Laguna Seca near Monterey to watch a car race. Memo didn't know anything about racecars, or the names of any of the drivers, but he was interested. When he came home he moved onto the boat with Cass to save money to go to the race car driver's training school. (In reality, the students worked on the cars and once a month got to drive them). I was hoping that he would become a mechanic and work on my car, but that was not his plan. He was set on being a racecar driver.

The first car race I went to was in Portland, Oregon. Memo qualified second. During the race there was a comfortable distance be-tween his car and the car ahead and also between him and the car behind. *Okay, just don't let them get any closer. Keep that same distance,* and that's what happened. He finished second. Sharon and I ran to the podium to see him receive his trophy. That was my son! I basked in his glory, experiencing a rush of good feelings towards racing.

Throughout the years Memo raced for many teams and at many venues. As Racecar Mama, I joined him at Road America in Wisconsin, Three Rivers in Quebec, Watkins Glen in upstate New York, Phoenix, Fontana, Long Beach, Mid-Ohio, Mexico City, and Vancouver Canada. There were memorable times, some good, some bad. I got a prescription for an anti-anxiety drug and sometimes just paced around behind the grandstand.

One year when Memo was racing a Champ car for the Target team, he and I were spending the night in a motel in Salinas. The track was Laguna Seca. This was during the years when Memo thought he was only able to sleep in a recliner. There was no recliner in the room, so late at night I went with him as he threw a lounge chair from the pool over the fence and carried it up to his room.

The next day there were 80,000 people at the track. I can't remember why, but Memo had to start last in a field of twenty-eight cars. My heart was pounding as I watched from the wooded area near the Corkscrew, a gnarly part of the track. Every time the cars came around, Memo had moved up a few positions, until finally he was second. He almost got around Michael Andretti who ended up first.

After the race I rode in a victory car with Memo and one of Memo's sponsors. We were driven around the track with 80,000 people cheering and applauding. Memo's friends had hung up a huge "GO MEMO!" banner and waved and cheered extra loud for him as we passed by.

This was one of the great moments of being Racecar Mama, but the next memory is not so happy.

It was January of 2014. I was in a wheelchair due to fracturing the bone outside of my hip replacement. I was being pushed in my wheelchair by my sister Patty on the bike trail by Blackie's pasture when Lupe called. She said that Memo was in an accident on the track during the 24 Hour Daytona race. She didn't know all the details. Those were revealed slowly over the next several anxious hours.

Memo was so looking forward to this race, happy to be in a car again after a dry spell. He had been doing extra workouts in order to be in the best possible shape. By nightfall the surgeons at the hospital had called me several times for my permission to do this and that kind of surgery or procedure on him. Two days later I was out of the wheelchair and catching a plane to Daytona Beach.

When I saw him in the hospital the night I arrived, his condition was shocking. He was immobile, with tubes running in and out of everywhere. His face was swollen and bruised, and he was semi-conscious. He mumbled a hello. He had fourteen broken bones and required five or six surgeries.

After two weeks in the hospital in Daytona Beach, Memo, his girlfriend Mari, and I were flown in a noisy little prop plane to a hospital in Santa Rosa. The flight in the middle of the night was a nightmare. The inside of the plane was cramped and freezing cold. Memo was in terrible pain, but the two paramedics on board could not give him any more morphine. We landed in a snowstorm in Waco, Texas to refuel, and then finally landed in a rainstorm in Santa Rosa. There was a bumpy and painful ambulance ride to the hospital.

Memo was in the Santa Rosa hospital for a few weeks. After that he spent a couple of weeks in a live-in rehab center in Oakland. Mari and I were his caretakers. She was his girlfriend at the time of his crash, but she stuck with him, and now they are married.

When he could finally go home to Sausalito, he underwent every kind of therapy possible and also did water-walking at the Jewish Community Center. He had many appointments at St. Mary's Hospital in San Francisco. His recovery was slow. We drove him around, and we walked with him. Milestones occurred when he was able to step from the dock onto our sailboat *Basic Instinct*, and when he could drive himself around in his car.

Three and a half years went by. He finally was able to put a helmet on again and climb into a racecar. It was a big deal. He took some laps around the track at Sears Point. Watching him I had mixed emotions. When Memo was a kid I had hoped he would become a professional tennis player.

DONUTS

It all started when Rachel was just a few months old. I would wheel her in an umbrella stroller from Memo's house in Novato to the shopping center. It was a good place for us to go. When Memo had work to do or was going to the gym or the track, I was in charge of Rachel. I was always looking to take her outside and to get moving.

When she was very little she slumped over in the cheap little stroller and I would wheel her the back way through the streets of the neighborhood where I would point out all the interesting sights and sounds—like the huge tree that was always packed with noisy birds and the sprinkler where the spray partially soaked the sidewalk. "Water, water, wet, wet," I would say when we felt the spray.

When I discovered there was a donut shop right near the Post Office in the shopping center that became our destination. I'd wheel her inside, park the stroller next to a booth, and order myself a cup of coffee and a raised sugar or chocolate donut. Then I'd lift her out of the stroller and set her down in the booth opposite me.

Rachel watched me placidly as I ate the donut and drank the

coffee. Memo, I knew, would say that donuts were not good for her, so I sat munching in peace with Rachel's big green eyes staring at me. Eventually I felt a little guilty.

"I don't think you'll choke on it," I said as I took off a tiny bit and put it into her pudgy little hand. She sucked it down, (I don't think she had any teeth at the time), and I finished the rest. The little tiny piece was all that she got, but she remembered. A few weeks later we went back to the donut shop. This time she put her hand out as I was eating my donut. Ok, so again I gave her just a little piece.

As time went on, the piece I had to give her got bigger and bigger and she would finish it before I ate my donut. Then I would have to give her two pieces when her hand came out. By the time she was three years old, I was cutting the donut in half, and it was "our" donut.

Each time her share got bigger and bigger and she consumed it quicker and quicker. Finally, I had to buy each of us a donut.

Rachel would stand in front of the case and point to the biggest one, with the most sugar and frosting on top. "No, only one of those little round ones," I told her. By the time Rachel was about six years old, she'd finish her donut first and would want a piece of mine.

We were hooked on donuts. One of my favorite stories as a kid was "Homer Price and the Donut Machine." The machine goes berserk and won't shut off so that thousands of donuts keep piling up. I got the book out of the library and read it to Rachel. Every time I took care of her we always had to get a donut.

Unfortunately, the pleasant Asian woman who ran the shop moved to North Carolina to be with her husband and left the store to her sister, whom neither Rachel nor I liked. The sister would not let me use the bathroom, which I needed after my cup of coffee. We stopped going there and had to look for a different donut shop.

My friend Mary Beth and I found a gourmet donut shop in San Rafael and met there from time to time to partake of a delicious donut treat. However, the last time we were there chatting, eating a donut, and drinking coffee, I pulled a stringy filament out of my donut. I held it up. "What's this?"

"Looks like dental floss," Mary Beth said.

"Yuck, dental floss?" Even though the employee quickly substituted a fresh donut, I lost my taste for donuts for a while.

But now I'm back on the donut kick. With Rachel and all my other grandkids the donut tradition is strong. We are always betting donuts for this or that reason, or I am using them as bribes. At last account, I owe a huge donut debt to Cassie, Ava, Rachel and Pia. Maybe I still owe donuts to my older grandkids, Riley, Hannah and Rosie too, but I think the statute of limitations has run out on them.

Donut tell your mother

THE RAFT REVISITED

When I was young I wanted to be a female Huck Finn. I wanted to drift on a raft down the Mississippi. What a great time I'd have, lazily going where the river took me, seeing new shores, meeting off-beat people like the characters in *Huck Finn*.

There is that saying, "Be careful what you wish for..." In 1973 at age thirty-five I signed onto a raft to drift across the Atlantic Ocean. Santiago Genoves the leader, was a charismatic Mexican anthro-pologist who hatched his raft idea after being on Thor Heyerdahl's *Ra I* and *Ra II*. They had drifted across the Atlantic on papyrus rafts.

Our voyage on the *Acali*, a few years after Heyerdahl's, lasted 101 days. Santiago called our raft a "floating laboratory." There were eleven of us guinea pigs. We left from the west coast of Africa and made it to Cozumel, Mexico despite hungry sharks, a freighter almost running us down, a hurricane in our path, and the mutinous plans of some of the participants.

Forty-three years later who would have thought that, at age seventy-nine, I would be reliving the journey on a replica of the raft in a film studio in Trollhätan, Sweden!

Marcus Lindeen, a young Swedish filmmaker, was the leader of the second *Acali*. He had read about the raft expedition in a book about the hundred most bizarre adventures in the world. Marcus got in touch with Maria, the Swedish captain of the original raft, and she helped him get in touch with those of us who were still alive.

At first, I ignored Marcus' emails. I deleted them as fast as they came until Maria urged me to respond. She said that Marcus was a "good guy and a successful filmmaker." She believed that he would make an "honest film" about the *Acali*. So I talked to him on the phone, and during the summer he came to my apartment to interview me and take clippings, notebooks, my movies, and some photos from the big old box labeled *Acali* that was in my closet.

The first time I flew across the Atlantic I remember looking down at the immense sea below me and thinking, *we are flying across this ocean in a matter of hours, but will be drifting back on a raft and barely moving!* When I flew across the Atlantic Ocean the second time it was with my oldest granddaughter Hannah. I told Santiago, (oops, I mean Marcus), that I could not manage at the advanced age of almost eighty to make the trip without Hannah as my caretaker. Besides, she had just graduated from film school and could be helpful in other ways.

Hannah enjoyed herself on the plane, drinking wine with two young men sitting next to us who were from Montenegro. I drank a little wine hoping that it would put me to sleep but it didn't. Even though I wasn't going to have to drift back, flying across the Atlantic in 2016 was torture.

Hannah and I arrived in Sweden during a snowstorm. We were picked up by Chu, the producer, and driven to Trollhätan from Gothenburg. There was little to see except snow falling and a gray and bleak-looking countryside. I was very tired, but I tried to make conversation with Chu. Hannah fell asleep in the backseat.

We were the first to arrive. When Marcus greeted us he informed me that I would have a wardrobe meeting that afternoon and later in the evening they would film an interview of me in the studio. I was so exhausted and jetlagged that I felt sick. I got through the wardrobe meeting, but before the interview, I started losing my voice.

By the time that Hannah and I met Marcus and the cameraman in the lounge, I could barely talk. Marcus' face fell. He sent me and Hannah to our flat with some throat lozenges and instructions to "get some rest and get your voice back." They would postpone my interview until the next day.

But I was still sick and in bed the next day. Marcus appeared at the door to check on my voice, I could only nod when he said, "We've got to get you talking again!" Two days later he sent me to a Swedish doctor with instructions to get me my voice back. Thank god for Hannah. She shopped for me, cooked for me, and truly was my caretaker. I was sick for more than a week.

One by one the other women from the raft arrived in Trollhätan. Maria, our Swedish woman captain, was a chain-smoking retired sea captain who was divorced and lived in a smoke-filled apartment up several floors of an old building in Gothenberg. Her apartment was filled with memorabilia from all the ports she had visited on freighter trips all over the world. The last night before flying home, three of us spent the night with Maria in her apartment. I slept with a woolen sock over my face trying not to breathe in air that reeked of cigarette smoke.

Fé, the other American woman had come to Trollhätan from Fairbanks, Alaska. She was the Black American on *Acali* who was supposed to be in conflict with me. In Sweden, she wore fluffy pink earmuffs and walked slowly due to bad knees and being overweight. I thought she exaggerated when she talked about some of the conflicts and incidents that occurred aboard the raft.

Edna, the raft's doctor from Israel, now lives in Germany. She was once again busy talking and ministering to us, the same as before. Servanne, the French frogwoman and swimmer, came to Sweden from Paris. I didn't really get to know her on the first raft because she was Santiago's mistress and loyal to him. When we met forty-three years later, I felt that I had the most in common with her.

When I had recovered enough to appear in the studio, I was told that there would be a surprise waiting there for me, and that it wouldn't just be seeing the replica of *Acali* for the first time. It was the appearance of Rachida. At first, I didn't recognize her, then of course I did. She was plumper, but still the beautiful Rachida with the same light in her eyes, exuberant sense of humor, and joyful laugh. It was Rachida in a sixty-five-year-old woman's body.

Fé, Me, Edna, Maria, Servanne

On my first day on the set Marcus wanted me to sit around the table of *Acali* with the others, but without talking. The film was supposed to take place all the same day so our clothes and our voices had to sound the same in every shot. I was not allowed to say anything in my cracking voice, only to sit and nod.

All six of the women made it to Trollhätan for the filming. Of the men, only Eisuke, our photographer, was there. Bernardo, the black Catholic priest from Angola was alive, but he had a heart condition and could not travel. The rest of the men—Santiago, Charles, and José Maria, had already passed away.

When Santiago lured people to go on the raft he was forty-eight years old. He was thirteen years older than me and even older than the other women and men of the raft. That didn't stop him from strutting around like a young man, sucking in the sea air, and puffing up like a rooster. He was a charismatic and handsome guy who thought all women found him irresistible. To make sure of the odds, he stocked the raft with six women and five men. One of the males was a priest, one was himself, and another was one of his students—slim pickings for us women.

In 2005 I called Santiago when I was in Mexico City for Memo's race. I wanted to see him, but he was too ill. He died in 2013.

Now it was 2016 and Marcus had finished filming. Before we left Trollhätan, Maria called me into her room. She had her doubts about what Marcus was going to "make of it all." She was afraid that he was not going to tell the truth either.

One of the scenes that Marcus wanted to record was the time of the "hurricane." He brought in a powerful wind-making machine and had each of us take a turn clinging to the rail of the raft as our hair was blown straight back. I had to hang on tight not to be knocked over by the force of the wind.

All this time Marcus was asking Fé to talk about the hurricane. Maria took me aside. "It vas not a hurricane, it vas just a squall." Then she shook her head and walked away.

Marcus gathered a ton of material. I couldn't imagine how he would be able to make an hour and a half film out of it. But he did.

Flash forward to 2019 when "The Raft" premiered in Europe and was widely acclaimed. When it came to San Francisco and San Rafael, I did Q&A's in front of sold-out audiences—which was more terrifying than drifting across the ocean. I am also featured in a three-part story in *Latitude 38*, a popular boating magazine, and in an hour long podcast on OutTheGateSailing.com. Being a celebrity was never my goal but what the heck…

BOATS AND DÉJÀ VU

It is June 4, 2016, and I discover that one doesn't forget how to sand and varnish a wooden boat. The best thing today about this boat, *Huck Finn*, is that it is a Bear boat and only twenty-four feet long. *Huck* belongs to the Sausalito Community Boating Center at Cass Gidley Marina. I am on the Board of Directors and I volunteered to help get it in shape. Margie, who races the boat, and my friend Charlotte are working on the boat with me.

Memo opted for fiberglass when we bought *Basic Instinct*, a thirty-five-foot sailboat. I was regretting that it wasn't wood, but he was right. Even so, Memo polishes and cares for it like it was a wood boat. He puts special polish on the stainless steel, a different polish on the cabin top, and a sealer on the teak in the cockpit, but that's nothing compared to the upkeep of a real wooden boat like the Bear which has twenty-four feet of bright work to keep up.

The *Tia Mia*, the twenty-eight-foot Friendship sloop that Cass and I owned, gave me my first experience sanding and varnishing a boat. There I was, a naïve young woman and the mother of Froggy varnishing the rails and cockpit, readying the boat for our maiden voyage to Mexico. I have a movie of Froggy, not yet two years old, sanding her potty chair. Her wispy blonde hair blows over her eyes and forehead. She looks up briefly, with a serious and all-business expression on her young little face, then looks back down and keeps working.

I grew up knowing a bit about sanding and painting because my father ran a barn painting business. He used to send me up on a one-hundred-foot high ladder to paint the white trim on the little windows of the cupola. The extension of the ladder was always narrow and springy. A small container of white paint was hooked over a rung of the ladder, then I began to paint. If I looked down, the cows and pigs were just pinpoints. The ladder swayed in the wind, not a nice feeling. I didn't want to admit that I was scared.

Cass was particular about the work done on the *Tia Mia* and the *Yo Ho Ho*. We used varnish remover to take off the old varnish. When it was applied, the old stuff curled up in dark yellow ribbons. Afterwards you scraped it off, being careful not to go too deep and gouge the wood. Then came the sanding.

First, you took a sheet of coarse sandpaper, folded it twice, creased the folds, then carefully tore the sheet into four sections. You folded one of the sections over four times and started sanding. When that section of sandpaper was smooth, you used a different side. Cass was picky. "Don't waste the sandpaper," he would say. The coarsest grade was 110, then came the 220, and finally the 440, which made the wood perfectly smooth.

After everything was sanded, you wiped the bare wood off and got all the fine dust away. Today Margie on the *Huck Finn* had some new hi-tech kind of cloth, but in the old days we just wiped the wood down with a rag dipped in turpentine, (which is probably toxic and illegal now).

Next it was time to pour the varnish, which was the color and consistency of Aunt Jemima syrup, into smaller containers. The varnish we used today looks the same to me, but then Margie handed me this little disposable foam thing for a brush! You didn't have to clean it, just throw it away?

It has been forty-five or more years since I moved off the *Yo Ho Ho*, and the world of boat maintenance has changed. I remember all of the toxic products that we were exposed to. Cass used sheets of asbestos to line the stove of the *Tia Mia* as well as the fireplace on the *Yo Ho Ho*. Asbestos particles floated in the air that we breathed.

We used turpentine, paint thinner, lead-based paint, and the dark red bottom paint, scraping and sanding it without even wearing a mask when the boat was hauled out. When I was pregnant I painted the crab buoys inside our salmon packing plant with no ventilation or mask.

Charlotte wore one of Margie's masks today that completely covered her nose and her mouth—even though we were working outside in fresh air with a light breeze.

There is a memory I have of sanding and varnishing the rails of the *Yo Ho Ho* on a Thanksgiving Day in San Diego. The kids and I were alone on the boat. I was wondering what the hell I was doing there and why I was doing it.

Cass was in Marin having lots to drink and a big turkey dinner with friends at the "Jezebel" woman's house. I was feeling stupid and resentful, maybe even crying. (Years later I heard that the "Jezebel" woman fell off a stool changing a light bulb when she was drunk and it killed her. Hmm...serves her right?)

ALCOHOL, MARY-JANE, AND ME

The first time I got drunk I was eighteen years old. Beer was legal at eighteen in Wisconsin and getting drunk was a rite of passage. Our house by the lake was on the corner and only a few blocks from the Shuffle Inn. Cars always had problems making the turn if the occupants were coming from the Shuffle Inn.

On my birthday my older sister Marilyn and four friends came with me to celebrate. We walked to the Shuffle Inn.

A pitcher of golden beer was set before me. Someone poured. The glass of beer had foam on top that was like the frosting on a birthday cake. The first glass was a toast to me. The beer tasted cool and lovely going down. I was feeling joyous inside as everyone sang the drinking song for me.

My personality changed. I was giggly and funny, and not at all awkward and shy like my normal self. We finished the pitcher and ordered another. I think I stood up and spoke. Any fears and inhibitions had disappeared. I don't remember walking home.

The next morning Michael, the boy who lived next door, wanted me to go carp fishing with him. That's the kind of activity that we did together. Of course I said that I'd go. I was still high from the beer I had drunk and feeling super powerful. I paddled the canoe as he stood in the bow with his spear ready to thrust it into any fat lazy carp swimming below. Michael was Tarzan and I was his Jane. It was

191

wonderful to be alive in this beautiful world. I felt like I could do anything. I had found the key to happiness. Nothing could stop me now.

When I was going to the University of Wisconsin we drank 3.2% beer in the Student Union, and sometimes Marilyn and I came home from classes slightly inebriated. We tried to act normal and not giggle too much in front of my parents and younger sisters.

A few years after that, Cass introduced me to serious drinking. He never used a shot glass, just dumped the whiskey in the glass. One of his drinks was a "Boiler Maker," which was Scotch with a beer chaser. In Eureka, he and I never went anywhere without at least a beer beforehand. Later on, in Mexico, we drank rum that came in a gallon bottle and bought Pacifico beer by the case. All the gringos especially those on boats drank heavily. At the American Ladies luncheon in La Paz a woman declared that alcohol destroyed brain cells so she wasn't drinking anymore, but the majority of us didn't seem to care.

One time when I flew to Mexico I rode in a cab from the airport with a couple that I'd met on the plane. They heard some of my stories of previous wild times in La Paz. When the cab driver dropped me off at the corner of Lupe's land, they saw the broken down little trailer that I was going to stay in and the barbed wire fence encircling the land. They were intrigued. "We hope to see you walking around town," they said.

The next day I made a date with Mac Shroyer to play tennis. We were going to play some doubles at his club later in the afternoon after it had cooled down.

In the morning I walked down the *malecon* to look around and see what was new in La Paz. It was already so hot that I was sweating in just my tank top and shorts. As I walked along I spotted my friends from the day before. We stopped to talk on the sidewalk next to a restaurant. There was a sign out front advertising 3x1 Margaritas.

"Hey, there's three of us. How about a Margarita?" the man said.

"Good idea," said his wife.

"Okay with me," I said. We sat down and ordered the drinks.

In a few minutes the waiter came back and put **three** giant-sized

Margaritas in front of each one of us. A total of **nine** Margaritas now sat on our table! *What? We were supposed to drink three each?* I thought briefly about the tennis match that I was playing with Mac that afternoon. But the Margaritas looked so cold and delicious—the glass sweating, the salt on the rim…and it was so damned hot.

There is a saying in AA, "a man takes a drink, the drink takes a drink, and finally, the drink takes the man." In my case the first one tasted very good, but after three of them I knew I was in bad trouble. When we left the restaurant, I could barely walk, much less play tennis.

Once I got to the Marina de La Paz, I took a very long shower. I stood with the cold water streaming over my head hoping to sober up. I got in my tennis clothes, but I was still in a daze when Mac picked me up.

I tried to play but it was no use. Mac never knew why I was so foolishly missing balls that day. The result was that I didn't get another invitation to play tennis with him for a long time.

I thought I had learned my lesson concerning alcohol and drugs, but recently, as an eighty-year-old, I overdosed on a brownie made with edible marijuana.

My doctor thought a little medical marijuana would help me sleep, reduce my headaches, and ease my anxiety. I recalled fondly the tasty little pot brownies that my sister made in the 60's. "It's worth a try," the doctor said, and gave me a letter enabling me to get a delivery of medical marijuana. I bought $50 worth, (which was the minimum amount for a delivery).

I forgot about my stash for a week or so, but one Sunday afternoon I decided to try some. I broke off two little tiny bits of special brownie about 12:30 p.m. and waited. Not feeling any effect by 1 p.m., I sliced off a second little sliver. This time when I looked out my kitchen window I noticed that the leaves and the trees were in 3D and I was feeling very strange. A few minutes later I couldn't do anything and I felt terrible.

I lay down on my bed, shoes still on because I had planned to do so much that afternoon. The sun was shining but I felt dizzy and weak, and my throat and mouth had a terrible taste. I felt horrible, wondering how long it would take to get over the effects of the brownie.

It got worse. I felt like I was going to die. I couldn't talk or walk. I sat rocking back and forth while sitting on the edge of the bed feeling nauseous. I wanted to call someone but I couldn't figure out how to do it. I texted an incoherent message to Memo, but he was out on a charter. I tried unsuccessfully to call Val, my friend who lives down the street.

Then I remembered Kevin, Val's son-in-law, who had been a drug counselor. I managed to get him on the phone and tell him that I'd overdosed, and that I thought I was going to die.

"You will live," he assured me. "You should feel better in thirty minutes. If you don't, call again and I will come by."

After thirty minutes I didn't feel better so I called him again and Kevin stopped in. I don't remember how long he was with me, but it was dark when he left. I remember rocking back and forth, rolling on the floor, and massaging my legs. I also lay on the foam roller and did yoga stretches while Kevin asked me questions. I think he was checking to see whether my brain was working.

We talked about Thanksgiving plans, his daughters' homework, pickleball, and Halloween costumes. Kevin was probably with me for at least three hours. I felt no pressure that he wanted to leave. He seemed happy just hanging out. Kevin is my hero!

The following day and a few days after, Kevin called and wondered how I was feeling. I told him how strange I still felt. It took a week for me to feel normal again. The rest of the brownie is now in the vegetable drawer of the refrigerator. I gave the other $50 worth of edibles to my grandson Riley for a birthday/Christmas present.

Riley didn't believe that the brownie that I overdosed on contained 1,000 mg's of marijuana. I took a close-up photo of the package with my phone and sent it to him.

"You weren't kidding!" he texted back.

Memo, Mother, and Lilly the lapdog

MY MOTHER DIED OF DEHYDRATION

My mother died of dehydration at the age of ninety-four. I saw the nurses at the hospice center pick her body up from the bed. It was floppy and limp, like a rag doll's. The women wrapped her in a patchwork quilt and sang "Amazing Grace" as they wheeled her out. My sister, niece, and I followed the procession out the door to the funeral home car.

In Meriter hospital, (before her stay in hospice), Mother suddenly started talking out of her head, accusing men of robbing her home in her absence. The truth was that a friend and I were cleaning out her house, pulling everything out of those million little cupboards in the kitchen, taking my father's fishing gear full of dust and mold out of the basement, and removing the rusty chain that was still around the post where my dog K.D. was always tied. Thinking that Mother would never make it back home, we were emptying the house so it could be sold.

It was a little freaky to me that she thought that people were taking her stuff. *How did she know what we were doing?*

My mother was not the most beloved patient at Meriter, although her mind was still as "sharp as a tack." She complained about the food and she complained about the staff. She wanted to get out of there. One of her biggest complaints had to do with the aides wheeling the patients out of their rooms and parking them in front of a large TV screen for hours on end.

"Why do they do that? Do they think we like sitting there doing nothing? Half of them fall asleep," she said. There was only one activity that she didn't grumble about. The physical therapist had the patients batting a balloon back and forth. My mother was good at it, and she liked it.

When I visited her I usually wheeled her outside, up and down the steep sidewalks near downtown Madison. One day I thought how easy it would be to accidentally lose my grip on the handlebars of the wheelchair and say "Whee!" and watch her careen down the street.

When my mother was no longer lucid, the staff finally stumbled on the notion that she was dehydrated. No one had been monitoring her fluid intake. She was transferred to the hospital unit to rehydrate her. They were trying to make her well enough to send her back to her room. She cried every time they tried to insert the IV. Her veins kept collapsing.

She wasn't getting better. My sister Mickey decided it was time to apply to hospice for a more pleasant place for my mother, and the doctor agreed. Later I found out that to be eligible for hospice one was supposed to die within ten days.

They transported my mother to the cheerful, serene hospice facility outside of Madison. Her room looked out on a patio with neatly tended gardens full of flowers and trees and with beautiful blue skies above. But my mother was too far gone to appreciate her surroundings.

My sister, my niece Kathleen, and I took turns staying with Mother in her room. She wasn't eating much, so when they brought in her tray, we usually ate her food. She soon lapsed into unconsciousness. One afternoon the priest came in and administered the last rites. Even though my mother no longer attended church, she was faithful about regularly sending in a donation.

One evening, my niece and I had a big scare. We thought that Mother was coming back to life. We were sitting in the room eating the pizza and the fresh strawberries on her tray. My mother must have smelled the pizza. Suddenly she sat up in bed and demanded to know what we were eating. When we told her, she said, "I want some strawberries, and maybe some bites of pizza too."

Kathleen and I almost choked on the half-chewed bites in our mouths as we hastened to get her some food. But Mother wasn't serious about coming back to life. Later that night she went back into a coma.

Early one morning a few days later, Mickey got the call. She had gone home instead of spending the night at hospice. Mother had passed away in the early hours. They waited until morning to call Mickey, and she waited a few more hours to call me.

I was staying in my mother's house and a strange thing had happened in the middle of that night. I was sleeping upstairs when I thought I heard something in the living room. I got up and felt my way downstairs in the dark, clinging to the bannister. I found no burglar, nothing amiss. I sat down in my mother's recliner that faced the picture window overlooking the lake. The lights of the Capitol building were still glowing. I watched them fade as dawn was starting to break.

A little bird unexpectedly flew up and landed outside on the window sill. The bird hopped back and forth and started tapping on the glass like it wanted to come in, (this bird was unusual because it had not flown into the window and gotten knocked senseless like so many other birds had done over the years).

Just at dawn, as the sun was starting to color the sky and the clouds, the little bird flew away. I went back upstairs to bed. A couple of hours later my sister called me to say that my mother had passed away at 5 a.m., the same time that the little bird had appeared to me.

I was sure then that the bird was my mother trying to get into her house one last time. Then her spirit had flown away.

MISS RITZMAN & WRITING

I'm happiest playing tennis, swimming, or writing. Tennis fills me with endorphins. The same for swimming and other outdoor activities. I need to be exercising to escape the gloomy self that comes from being closed in with no fresh air and no blood moving.

For my brain to be happy, writing is the key. When I was a kid and felt angry, hurt, or sad, I'd run upstairs, fling myself on the bed, and write about my feelings. I've done it all my life. I have boxes and boxes full of old steno pads and notebooks filled with my secret unpublishable thoughts. My granddaughter Hannah has been instructed to burn them when I die.

In grade school we didn't do any writing except for exercises in penmanship. I remember how happy I was when we finally got a writing assignment in the eighth grade. I wrote a funny piece about my sisters and my dog.

At Central High School there was an English teacher named Miss Ritzman who all the kids feared. She had a reputation of being too demanding and strict. Everyone in the school would say, "Oh no! You got her for English?" She was my English teacher for all four years.

Miss Ritzman was an awesome force and power, and she was quite overweight. With peroxided hair, bright red lips, and dangly noisy bracelets she looked like a carnival gypsy. I trembled when she walked by my locker. I was afraid of her, but she liked me and what I wrote.

The first assignment we had in ninth grade was to analyze the woman's role (Kate's) in *Taming of the Shrew*. In my paper, I deplored the idea of Kate jumping up to fulfill every whim and command of her husband. (This was way back in 1951, long before women's lib). Miss Ritzman read my theme aloud to the class and gave me an A+. She chastised the other students for their unsatisfactory work as she handed my paper back to me. She smiled at me. Suddenly she knew who I was.

Miss Ritzman instructed us from a lectern in the front of the room. Sometimes when she lectured I drew sketches of her, fascinated by her larger-than-life person. She wore big earrings and bright bracelets. The flab under her arms shook and jiggled when she wrote on the blackboard.

When I was in tenth grade Miss Ritzman singled me out to write the commentary for the halftime show at the football game. We were a downtown school so the games were played under the lights at a stadium called Breese Terrace. I played trombone in the marching band, and we always put on a half-time show.

As we made a "C" formation on the field in our orange and black uniforms, I heard the words I'd written over the PA system. They ended with "that Miss Ritzman, she sure throws a lot of weight around here…"

She let them say that over the loudspeaker! For the entire student body and teachers to hear!

On one of my themes Miss Ritzman had commented "You should try your hand at writing. You have a knack for it." On another paper she had written, "Live up to what you know." When we were due for new band uniforms Miss Ritzman nominated me to be on the committee. She was head of the committee. I met in the office with her and another teacher and two other students, but I was way too uncomfortable to say anything.

When I was in my senior year, there was a handsome new male teacher named Mr. Besant who taught English and French. He and Miss Ritzman began walking down the hall together, laughing and talking like lovebirds. He was about thirty years old, while Miss Ritzman was around fifty. It was a scandal. He was also married! (Miss Ritzman, like almost all of my teachers through high school were "old maids"). How we students gossiped about them!

Just before graduation, Miss Ritzman invited a few senior girls in her class to have tea with her. The experience was almost as bad as going to the Senior Ball. I wore a skirt, high heels, and sat tongue-tied, nervously shaking my cup and trying not to spill the tea.

After I left high school, Miss Ritzman would appear in my dreams now and then. One day about fifteen years later, a vaguely familiar man walked into Howard Johnson's where I was working as a waitress. He sat in the bar and told me his name was Mr. Foster. He had been Marilyn's English teacher at Central High School. I served him a drink and he reminisced. He asked me if I knew that Miss Ritzman had died.

"No, I didn't know that." I said. "She was my favorite teacher."

"Poor woman," he said, "did you know that she was a virgin her entire life?" Then he had another drink.

It didn't surprise me. No man wanted as intelligent and over-powering a woman as her in those days. She was not at all like Kate in *Taming of the Shrew*. (I think I was like Kate with Cass, despite what I wrote in ninth grade).

✧

At the University of Wisconsin, I took a creative writing course. The story the instructor liked the best was about Michael, the boy next door who was in love with me. The instructor encouraged me to send it to a magazine. I sent it to *Seventeen*, but they wanted me to revise the ending, which I took as a rejection.

At the UW, I followed Marilyn's footsteps and majored in journalism. After graduation I got a job as a reporter in Eureka, writing news stories and feature articles for the *Humboldt Times and*

Standard. I wrote obituaries, church page stories, and wedding stories too. After I married Cass I wrote some articles on our family's sailing adventures on the *Tia Mia* for *Sea Magazine,* and for *The Independent Journal,* Marin County's daily newspaper, but most of the time I was too busy to do much writing.

My next writing, later in life, was screenwriting at College of Marin. The teacher, Sandy Handsher, was a tough, demanding woman, (another Miss Ritzman). I went to the class not having registered for it. The class was full, but then she sent us out in pairs to write a scene using some overheard dialogue. I was eager to do it. The woman I was paired up with was not as enthusiastic, in fact she and some other students decided not to come back. That's how I got in the class.

Upon returning to the classroom there was another test. She wanted us to write down five of our favorite movies. I wracked my brain. During the years we were living on the boat I hadn't seen a movie, except for the premiere of *The Ten Commandments.*

Let's see *Bambi?* Would they laugh at me? *La Strada, My Friend Flicka, The Greatest Show on Earth,* and *The Yearling.* Whew, that's five.

Our first homework assignment was to write a treatment for a movie—to put up our sleeves and get to work. Again, I was one of those who did it. My story was about a commercial fisherman and a young naïve newspaper woman, and the sinking of the fisherman's boat. All these characters and the plot were more or less based on Cass and me and the commercial fishing scene, which was all so true and close to my heart. The screenplay was called *Jack,* (AKA *Staying Afloat* or *Shit Happens*).

Sandy Handsher urged me to send it to a national contest, and also to *Playhouse 90,* a popular TV show. The comments I got back were positive, but nobody liked the ending (mainly because the dog died). An agent told me to write it as a novel first, then she would represent me. I didn't do it and gave up trying to sell it.

During the past thirty years I've written five screenplays, a dozen or more short stories, some poetry, several essays, and a one-act play. I also wrote an article about Mac and Mary Shroyer of the Marina de La Paz for *Latitude 38.* One of the screenplays was a collaboration with my friend Savannah. She recently resurfaced in my life and now we are collaborating on another screenplay. It's not easy though because she lives in Boise, Idaho.

After twenty years of not being in contact, with Sandy Handsher, my old screenwriting teacher, we reconnected. Last summer we met at a restaurant in San Rafael where I had coffee and a pastry, and she ate a big healthy salad. We caught up on each other's retirement years and ailments. Then she pestered me about my needing to get an agent in order to sell my stories and screenplays.

"In all my 28 years of teaching, your screenplay *Wundersea* was the best," she said.

That felt almost as good as if I had sold it.

OLD AGE WITHOUT A DOG

A few years ago I told my family that I didn't want any presents for my birthday, I just wanted homemade cards. One of my young granddaughters drew grass, birds, and butterflies on the outside of her card. On the inside she wrote, "Happy birthday, Grandma. Now you are as old as dirt." It reminded me of a card that my Val received from her daughter. It read, "Now that you've reached the age that you've always dreaded becoming..."

Yes, I'm definitely on my way to becoming dirt. Sometimes I'm proud of it. When I kicked butt at tennis last season, I rubbed it in by saying, "You know what, I'll be 82 next month."

I never thought I would live this long. It seemed like 80 would be an acceptable and normal age to cash it in. But now that I am 82, I'm thinking ahead to, maybe 90.

I have some random thoughts about aging. Number one, when you get older it is difficult to hang on to a sense of humor. I read that both James Thurber, and Mark Twain, whom I admire for their writing and sense of humor, became cranky and bitter in their old age. My mother also comes to mind, although she is a special case because she was cranky and negative most of her life.

I attribute some of this lack of a sense of humor to the aches and pains of old age, also the difficulty of getting a good night's sleep. It's not easy to be happy and chipper when you are sleep-deprived.

The gravest medical condition that I now have is called "myelopathy of the cervical spine." This past summer a doctor showed me the MRI that revealed my unprotected spinal column. The advice I was given was "don't fall," and "don't get in a car accident." The result of a blow to my head or a fall could be paralysis from the neck down or dying instantly. Did the doctors also say, "Don't play tennis?" I can't remember. Probably they did, but I've started playing again anyway. I've been told that surgery is an option, but it is a risky operation that is not always successful.

When I got the news, I was thinking that I better do the Advanced Care Directive that Kaiser has been asking of me, and when I got home, I mentally started deciding who would get what of my most prized possessions. I thought of my grandson Riley for my grandfather's pitch pipe, my friend Frank for my metal basket of tennis balls, my granddaughter Hannah for the wine-colored bulky sweater that my sister knitted for me, my son Memo for my mother's 100-year-old toaster, and daughter Sharon or sister Patty for my Santa Claus bulbs from the 1930's.

I don't know who would want my 50-year-old couch or my 1973 Kenmore vacuum cleaner. The Goodwill people already rejected the couch. I don't know whether I can handle any more rejections.

Now that I'm on the subject of "things," I have an aversion to acquiring new things because I don't like having to throw old things away. I am afraid that they will end up in the landfill. It's also true that new things are cheaply made and are not manufactured to live very long, unlike my good ol' toaster and vacuum. To throw away things is the hallmark of capitalism. President Bush once called our throw away society non-negotiable. It is our AWOL (American Way of Life).

I think I've been lucky to have lived in the "good old days." When I was young the U.S. went to war in a "good war" that lasted about four years. We only had one A-bomb to worry about, not thousands of nuclear warheads. We never thought about pollution—we burned our trash in a big barrel in the vacant lot. There were no traffic jams and no freeways. We didn't worry about population growth or greenhouse gases, and plastic was a new thing. We didn't have TV, Gameboys, computers, cell phones, Facebooks, leaf blowers, or digital anything to distract us from living.

Although I say that I hate computers, it was a pleasant surprise when I first used one for word processing. I could delete wrong words, change spelling, move paragraphs around with no more crossing out or erasing…wow! However, I still prefer a real piece of paper and a good pen or a sharp pencil for writing or doodling, and I admit to being technologically challenged. My granddaughter Rachel was shocked when she found that out. "An app, Grandma? You don't know what an app is?"

We had telephones, but it was a party line, which meant that someone could be listening in or waiting to make a call. Our first phone number in Madison was Badger 7049. When you picked up the receiver, you got the operator, who connected you to the number you were calling. There were no long conversations.

Most everybody seems to think that "progress" and "techno-logy" are desirable. The science writer Isaac Asimov claimed that any of the bad effects of technology could be solved by creating a new technology. Huh!

At age 82, I wonder how much of who I am is due to my natural born temperament and personality, and how much of me is the result of my mother's influence. From her I learned to clam up, fade away, shut up, to listen and never say what I really thought, and to not ask questions. I also was bathed in negativity.

The bold "other Mary" has come out on occasion. A few years ago, when planning the girls' tennis team party, head coach Charlie wanted me to interrupt him as he was talking. I should tell him to sit down and shut up because he had said enough. Well, I did! The girls and their parents looked at me in shock and amazement. The alter-ego self of mine had come on powerfully strong.

Was that the real me or was I acting? Am I really forceful, opinionated, and outspoken? It was a great feeling to have this "other Mary" take over for a change. Later I noticed that the girls and parents who were at the party kept a wary eye on me.

Another time when my alter-ego surfaced was at Hannah's high school graduation party. I danced my head off, celebrating with abandon like a natural born party animal. Also, at Memo and Mari's wedding, I popped up and asked to give a toast (which the normally reticent Mary would never have done).

Enough said. I have decided that from now on I will be the forceful, outspoken, fearless Mary...starting... now!

I just finished Daniel Quinn's autobiography *Providence* which is as entertaining and profound as his book *Ishmael.* I strongly believe that this country and the world is going to hell. Quinn writes that the only way to save this planet is to get rid of the Taker story, in which the planet belongs to Man, and to base all our actions on the story that the Leavers were enacting, that Man belongs to the earth.

Myself, I am a natural born Leaver. I don't believe in God, I believe in evolution. My religion is animism (that the life force is in everything, and humans are not special). Now that I understand this about Leavers and Takers, I can't get too excited about politics. I don't feel the need to call Congress or to send money to Bernie Sanders' campaign. The entire premise that has brought us to this point is wrong and had its beginnings 10,000 years ago. Don't take my word for it, read *Ishmael.*

There is a popular opinion being promoted that if you are elderly and living alone you need to get a dog. I am not buying into it. My neighbor downstairs has a service dog. It's an annoying little pug that she "tells her troubles to." What's wrong with a stuffed animal like my Spot, or my Leo the lion? I can just as well talk to them, and there's no noisy barking or poop to pick up.

The last "pet" I had was a plastic goldfish of unknown origin. The good thing about Goldie was that I never had to feed her and I rarely changed the water in the bowl. Goldie, however, tended to lie sideways on the top of the water. When someone came to visit, they would say, "Your goldfish looks kind of sick." I would answer, "Actually she's dead. It's plastic."

If you don't get a dog, then you should get a man? I've thought about it and recently almost let one into my house. But luckily the romantic feelings wore off before I did.

Sometimes I wish I did have someone to talk to and share my life with. In my younger days I wanted to have a man under my bed that I could call up when I wanted him. One day I was talking to a friend of mine whose husband went to Tahoe on business for a week. She was lamenting that he was away and I thought what a good relationship they must have. Then she said, "I miss Fred. He puts the gas in my car and does all the grocery shopping."

Aha, so that's it.

This concludes "Old Age Without a Dog" (or a man), and this is the end of my memoirs, except for the smatterings of poetry, short stories, and photos that follow.

As far as my wild life goes, I intend to take it easy from now on.

Que le vaya bien!

ONE FINAL NOTE

Point to Point will end on a sad note. My sister Mickey, youngest of the five Gartland girls, died unexpectedly after the first printing of this book. We had been estranged since my mother died in 2005. I had written that when I finished my memoirs I wanted to see about getting together with her again. I waited too long.

Mickey was a sensitive and dramatic soul who had her ups and downs, but I assumed she would be around when I was ready to resume our relationship. Now I will not see her again, not even to say goodbye.

She will be missed by all that knew and loved her.

A LITTLE POETRY

THINGS I'LL MISS

I'll miss thunder
the smell of first rain
puddles and mud
my old down pillow
waking up from a dream
rainbows on my walls
a good yawn
stretching my legs
the smell of fresh coffee.

I'll miss sunlight
ripples on the water
ocean waves
wiggling my bare toes in the sand
running for no reason
sweating
the popping sound of a clean volley
an icy cold beer.

I'll miss hugging people
groves of old Redwood trees
good ink pens
words
picking my nose
eating the edge of a muffin
floating in a tub of hot water.

And I'll miss breathing.

ALICE

There once was a woman named Alice
Who wanted to live in a palace
She married a drunk
Fell into a funk
And her dream went up in a chalice

PORK

There was a young man from New York
Allergic to all kinds of pork
But he found on his plate
Some bacon too late
And he died with some still on his fork

LAP DOG

I had an old lap dog named Fluff
Who would chew on my clothes and my stuff
I once got so mad
I spanked him real bad
Then he sunk his aged teeth in my duff

Poor Fluff, the vet's verdict was rough
He said he's got rabies sure 'nuff
Dog's death made me sad
But now I am glad
'Cause Fluff makes a wonderful muff

GOLDFISH

I had a young goldfish named Flo
Who once jumped out of her bowl
I was in a bad mood
(and out of fish food)
So I squished her with my big toe

MY COFFEE CUP

I slide it easily over the table

On the inside,
Old brown stains mark
coffee tides going in and out

Putting my hand over the brim,
Steam leaks through my fingers

Hooking my thumb into the handle,
I take control of the companion
that gives me so much—

The necessary transfusion,
The early morning consolation
for waking up again

DEEP PLEASURE IN THE POOL

I feel
pencil thin
stretched out and streamlined
garfish thin
about six feet long and snaky

I am quick
fast and strong
I am a happy thing

I am a sleek creature
with a rat tail that weaves behind me

The water gushes over
my every cell
I feel my heart beat loudly

I'm a hot-blooded woman
with wetted flesh
as I charge on through the water

But I swim with a secret
in the wavy blue
as you watch with admiring eyes

The secret is I am an old,
old creature
you see only the bubbles and smiles

THE SUDDENESS OF A SANTA ANA

Ripples on the dark foreboding sea
bouncing tops, giggling, happy travelers
chop, waves, froth,

a grimace
as water runs down the back
of his cold yellow slicker
like an unwanted ice cube

The wind and sea erupts
mast groans
a crash below

thrown to the opposite side
the first mate comes unglued

Waves in the frying pan
slop spaghetti over its banks
portholes swirl like laundromat doors

she looks up at his distorted face
for hope

He wrestles the beast
riding the humping bull
that slaps him with stinging sharp
spray

so much wind and water
God's let the hose go
and it's out of control

All hell above
All hell below

MOVING DAY

They carry her out past my window
I could have
shut
the blinds

"Goodbye Old Jessie," I whisper
as she comes by

They can't get her round the corner
so straight and
stiff
she lie

An unwieldy piece of furniture
they curse and
jostle
the bier

They tip it sideways and upside down
and bounce it
down
the stair

The body bag comes unzipped in my mind
"You can leave her here," I cry.

RIDING THE BUS IN A CULTURE WHERE THERE ARE VULTURES AND NOBODY CARES EXCEPT ME

On a refrigerated bus, bodies
speeding through the desert,
heavily curtained windows,
people in a stupor, curled up sleeping

Oddly cracked windshield
where a crucifix dangles
over the driver's dark head,
the Jesus figure dances
like a maniac when we hit deep ruts,

215

When we swing around a corner
I hold my breath
wondering
did the windshield get cracked
before or after
the crucifix was hung,

I don't trust God!

Roaring down a road, so narrow
and slim
that you can't see it,
stop briefly
at dusty crossroads,
taking on more souls
with sacks of food
and a sleeping bag for the journey,

God knows where they'll sleep
when they get to the border

Dodging cars, trucks and mines
veering past a cow
bus almost hits a shrine
spilling flowers and candles
on the ground

Across the aisle
a smiling ranch hand
reading a porno comic book,
drooling over hips and lips,
unconcerned about the crucifix
or the cracked window

When the bus crashes
a field of shrines will mark
the smoking ruins
where you all died.

Bring on the elephants!

SOME STORIES OF MEXICO
(and one about the Raft)
URBANO

Urbano was about 12 years old the first year we met him—a handsome smiling Mexican kid in bare feet and cutoffs who would appear out of nowhere whenever we rowed ashore. He would help us pull the skiff up on the beach and unload the kids and the dogs and the garbage and the water jugs and the crates of Vita sodas. Then he would ask what we needed to buy and where we needed to go.

He spoke a little English and he was not shy. He would get a younger boy to watch the skiff for us and then he would accompany us on our errands. We paid him a few pesos.

The first time we went ashore in La Paz, after sailing down the Baja peninsula, we felt like aliens from another planet.

When we walked down the dusty streets carrying baby Sharon, women would come up to us and take her from my arms. They would pass her around, admiring her wispy blonde hair, her blue eyes, and her fat cheeks. "*Qué chula, qée linda, qué preciosa,*" they would say and carry her away into their houses.

The first time she disappeared I was a little nervous, but Urbano seemed to think it was okay.

After a time Sharon would reappear in someone else's arms with candy dripping from her mouth. Then we would set off on foot again.

We had no idea where anything was and there was no one-stop shopping. We didn't know where the *panadería* was, we had no idea where to buy ice, or screws, or paper towels. Urbano helped us locate everything, except the paper towels.

Instead of paper towels, a shopkeeper would produce toilet paper, wax paper, napkins, or the coarse brown paper that they used to wrap purchases in, but not "*toallas de papel.*" They would shrug their shoulders and Urbano would take me on to the next store. (It turned out that paper towels didn't exist in La Paz in those days and the next year we brought a case down with us.)

We flew home in the spring, leaving the boat on a mooring in front of Jose's shipyard. The next year, Urbano was there on the beach again. The following year, when Lupe was due to be born, we drove down the mainland to do some more cruising, and Urbano was still there.

Urbano was not only the most helpful kid, he also could amuse Sharon, who was now almost four years old, by popping his cheek out, and putting his fingers in his mouth and emitting a high-pitched shrieking whistle. He also did something with his ears that would make her laugh uproariously.

Huckleberry was in love with him too. He would trot alongside Urbano with a stick in his mouth waiting for Urbano to toss it for him. Sometimes Urbano would drop down on all fours and bark like a dog and begin playing with Huckleberry.

We didn't understand why Urbano wasn't in school. Of all the kids who hung out at the beach by the shipyard, he seemed the sharpest and the most personable. He told us that he was finished with school because he had already graduated from the sixth grade. Little by little we got to know more. He came from a large family and his father worked for customs. There wasn't a lot of money.

We wanted to do something for him, maybe bring him back with us and put him in school. He told us that in the past other people on yachts had promised him the same thing, but it had never happened. Cass vowed that we would not disappoint him.

We left it up to Urbano to get all his papers together so he could go with us when we left La Paz in April. It would take us about a week to drive back to Sausalito. It was the second year that we had come by car down the mainland to Mazatlan and taken the ferry across the Sea of Cortez to La Paz. We towed an Apache tent trailer behind us and slept in it at night.

On the day of departure, the Tia Mia was buttoned down and covered with canvas, the mooring checked by a diver, and we said goodbye to José and our other friends. Urbano was with us, grinning ear to ear like the Cheshire cat. He was now part of our family. His black hair was neatly parted and slicked down. He wore a new shirt and pants and had on a pair of shoes.

The car we drove was a Mercedes diesel. Huckleberry was trained to ride in the tiny space in the folded up tent trailer that we towed behind it. The men at the shipyard had drilled extra holes in the door for him. Our shore boat, the Sabot, was lashed on top of the tent trailer and inside of it was all our diving gear, (although we never did much diving after the time that Cass jumped in with all the weights on him and there wasn't any air in the tank).

If Urbano was expecting a high class life with us gringos, he was mistaken. Once underway, the trip up was another experience in roughing it and getting by as cheaply as we could. At the end of a day we would head off into the sunset and set up camp in the middle of the desert. We cooked canned stew and fried potatoes and Spam on a camp stove and ate off tin plates.

Although friends had warned us of banditos, we no longer worried about being attacked and robbed or killed. We had slept peacefully for many nights in the middle of the desert in Mexico.

After a few days driving, we reached the road that cut across the state of Northern Baja and ended up at Tijuana and San Diego where we would cross the border. I checked our documents. Yes, they were all here, as well as the health certificate for Huckleberry. I asked Urbano if he had his papers. "Yes, I do have them," he said in his carefully enunciated, heavily accented English.

The next day we were stopped by Mexican officials at a station near Tijuana where he had to give up our tourist cards. They asked who Urbano was, and that is when we got the news that he did not have the right documents.

According to these Mexican authorities, he would not be able to enter the U.S. We climbed up the rickety stairs into an office above the checkpoint and asked the *jefe* what we could do about it. He looked at Urbano's papers gravely.

"You will have to drive him back to La Paz," he said. Cass reached in his pocket for his wallet, but the *jefe* shook his head. "*Es una cosa de los estados unidos. Qué lástima,,*" he added, unwilling or unable to take a bribe.

We drove back out of town in bad spirits and looked for a place to camp. Driving Urbano back to La Paz was out of the question. The commercial fishing season was opening in mid-April and as

219

operators of a commercial fish dock, we had to be back. We also didn't have enough money to fly him back home.

Sharon picked up that something was wrong. She wanted Urbano to make some funny faces and some funny sounds for her as Cass and I talked about what to do.

We couldn't understand why Urbano's father, who worked in customs, wouldn't have known what papers he needed. When we asked Urbano, he didn't know either. Then Urbano remembered that he had an uncle who worked at the border. When we asked him for his uncle's name, he drew a blank. We were skeptical. Anywhere he went in Mexico, Urbano probably had an uncle.

We went to bed. We would try to figure out what to do in the morning. We would probably have to put him on a bus and send him home.

In the middle of the night, I woke up to the sound of footsteps. I heard more footsteps and they sounded closer. I was terrified. Huckleberry who was sleeping outside under the tent began to whine.

"There's somebody out there," I said, shaking Cass. He sat up in bed and reached for the flashlight.

I dove back into my sleeping bag and hugged Sharon and Lupe to me. Any minute, I thought, I would feel a knife in my back.

"Huckleberry, sic 'em boy, go get 'em, boy," Cass ordered.

But Huckleberry continued to whine and tried to come into the tent. Cass shoved him back outside. Everybody was awake now. By now we could hear the heavy breathing of our attackers, but so far nothing had happened.

It was Urbano who finally had the courage to unzip the tent flap and peer out. Meanwhile, we scrambled to find anything we could use to defend ourselves.

Suddenly Urbano started yelling, "*Váyase, pendejos, váyase,*" and then he leaped out of the tent. We thought he must be crazy and that the banditos would surely kill him.

When Cass looked out, there was Urbano waving his arms, stamping his feet, and yelling…at a bunch of cattle.

Much relieved, we all joined in trying to scare the four-legged *banditos* away. When it was all over, we went back to sleep, impressed with Urbano's bravery.

In the morning we decided, what the hell, to head for the border. Maybe the uncle would appear and we could plead our case. The worst thing that could happen would be that they would turn us back.

We went through the car, the trailer, the boat, and the food box, dumping out our fruit and cleaning up a bit. I rinsed out some dirty diapers of Lupe's and shoved them in a bag.

We got a late start. Cass was driving and Urbano was sitting next to him in the front seat in case he spotted his uncle.

All of us were travel-weary and nobody was saying much. Sharon and I were in the back seat, playing with some paper dolls and fanning ourselves, and Lupe was asleep in her plastic clothes-basket on the floor of the back seat.

Although Urbano was sitting tall and erect and smiling serenely, I saw that the corners of his lips were twitching.

It was a hot Sunday afternoon and we got into Tijuana just as the bullfight was letting out. We got in a long line of cars heading for the border—bumper to bumper traffic going back to the States.

Most of the cars, which had just been in Tijuana for a day, were being waved through. When they saw our car, a man in a uniform diverted us to another location for customs and immigration. Another guy in uniform and sunglasses started walking toward the car.

But Cass didn't wait. He jumped out of the car quickly and went to the back of the trailer. He opened up the trailer door and Huckleberry leaped out. The official did a double-take seeing a big Airedale come out of the tiny space. Cass had the guy's attention. Cass demonstrated how the tent trailer worked and showed him what was in the skiff on top of the car. Then Cass got him interested in the diesel engine of the car. They both looked under the hood and talked some more.

While Cass was putting the hood down, the man walked back to the car. I thought the jig was up.

He asked for our vaccinations cards, which I handed to him. So far he had not said anything about the dark-haired, dark-eyed Mexican sitting in the front seat. When he handed the four cards back with no comment it suddenly dawned on me that he might not have counted Lupe who was asleep in her plastic clothes basket on the floor.

But he wasn't through with us. He leaned his head in the window and started sniffing.

"Do I smell any fruit in here?' he asked. I said I didn't think so. I saw Urbano open the glove compartment and prayed that he would not open his mouth.

"Nothing here," he said in his very limited English.

"It must be the dirty diapers in the back seat that you smell," I said quickly.

The officer retracted his head and did some fast paperwork. Then he walked away and waved us on. Cass put Huckleberry back in the trailer and got into the car. He started the engine and we drove away. We couldn't believe our luck. He had just let us through as though Urbano were invisible.

All the way to San Diego we kept looking behind us, expecting to see the Border Patrol coming after us with their guns firing. When we finally realized that we were free, we were ecstatic.

That night we went to some friends' house in San Diego for dinner and slept in the camper in their driveway.

We retold the border-crossing story to our hosts at dinner. They shook their heads in amazement, but told us we weren't home free yet. They told us that the Border Patrol sets up random check points all along Highway 101 trying to catch illegal aliens who have snuck through.

Not wanting to take any chances, we put Huckleberry in the front seat of the car and Urbano crawled into the back of the trailer.

We never were stopped, but Urbano rode back there all the way to San Francisco. He said it was a little bumpy, but the air holes gave him plenty of fresh air.

Huckleberry was quite happy with the arrangement.

THE TALE OF LEROY

When I was in La Paz one time a group of well-meaning gringos called "Las Mascotas" de La Paz were having a bake sale at the marina. They were raising money for a campaign to control the animal population of the city by getting people to neuter their dogs and cats. They also wanted to build an animal shelter.

I spent a few pesos on some cookies and a slice of carrot cake and thought of how different life had become in La Paz and I thought of LeRoy, *a mascota*, we once had. One of the most horrible images that I live with is that of my daughter Sharon's tear-streaked, grief-stricken face on the night that our cat, LeRoy, was killed.

LeRoy was given to my children as a kitten and was named before we found out it was a girl. At the time we were living on our boat, the *Yo Ho Ho*, in Sausalito, while preparing to head back to Mexico. Our good-natured Airedale, Huckleberry, accepted the cat because LeRoy acted more like a dog than a cat. She was an active little tiger kitty and the kids loved their new playmate. When she was older we intended to get her spayed.

The summer was nearly over and the *Yo Ho Ho* was not anywhere near ready to sail. I was eight months pregnant with a third baby, and since we wanted to have the baby in Mexico, it was decided that the girls and I would fly down to La Paz and Cass would join us later. He promised Sharon and Lupe that he would bring Huckleberry and LeRoy with him when he flew down for the baby's birth.

They gave their pets big hugs and we said goodbye. Sharon was seven years old and Lupe was four.

The girls and I arrived in La Paz in mid-August. When the stewardess opened the door of the air-conditioned plane, I didn't want to step outside. The heat was intense, like walking into a sauna or steam bath. I couldn't breathe.

Mary Shroyer picked us up in her jeep and whisked us off to her house before I could change my mind. She had a well in their yard with some water in it and I survived by sitting in it like a big pregnant walrus in my flowered bathing suit. We stayed with Mary and her family for about a week until she found us a house to rent down by the beach.

It was a medium-sized house surrounded by a large dirt yard and a wire fence. From the front yard you could walk down to the water. Cass could anchor the boat right out in front of the house. The house, though in the outskirts, was close enough to the school and some little stores. For $80 a month it was just fine.

In the front yard there was a cot. Because the nights were unbearably hot, I slept there with an assortment of bug, ant, and cucaracha spray cans lined up on the ground under my bed.

In the area surrounding the house lived many poor Mexican families, their tiny houses semi-hidden behind the scrubby trees and brush. Once my children started attending school, a large population of children and dogs from the neighborhood would follow them home. Most of the dogs were mean-looking brutes named Lobo or Diablo, and I would try to shoo them away.

After school the house and yard would be full of children playing games or drawing and coloring in the back room. Within a week my children were no longer drawing American looking trees or houses, but palm trees and brightly colored thatched roofed houses.

As promised, Cass flew in just before my son was born bringing Huckleberry and LeRoy with him. We had a specially built plywood box with Huckleberry's name and a dog's head on the side of the box and some air holes. Cass decided that the two animals could fit in the same box. When they arrived at the La Paz airport the Mexicans were surprised to see a cat and a dog leap out of it.

Huckleberry was an immediate hit with the Mexican kids. He was wary of the Mexican dogs, however, and kept one eye on them as he tirelessly retrieved sticks. LeRoy the cat learned to run up a tree whenever a dog got in the yard. She liked to chase the cucarachas in the kitchen.

Now that LeRoy was almost a full grown cat, we decided that it was time to have her neutered. The problem was that in Mexico who would perform this type of operation? Once again, Mary Shroyer came to our rescue. She gave us the name of a veterinarian who said he could do it. In the meantime, my son was born.

Shortly after the birth, Cass went back to Sausalito. It was up to me to carry through with the plan of getting LeRoy neutered. I made a date at the vet's for the end of October. Unfortunately, the date of a Halloween party that we had planned coincided with the exact date of LeRoy's operation.

The kids were terribly excited about having the party. They invited all the Mexican children in the neighborhood and told them to dress up. I invited the Shroyers and anybody else who wanted to come.

When it came time to think about our costumes, Sharon chose to dress up as an old lady. She would wear a print dress with an apron tied around her middle and borrow a wig and an old hat with a black veil and some glasses and carry an old purse of mine.

My costume was easy. I would wear my bright red maternity dress and make myself some cardboard horns. I would carry a rake, paint black marks on my face, and be the Devil. The baby, barely a month old, would be a ghost dressed in one of his long white sack nighties. (Sharon wanted to cut holes for his eyes in a diaper and cover his head too, but I vetoed the idea). Lupe would wear an old grass skirt and put flowers in her hair and be a Hawaiian dancer.

We planned to go all out for this Halloween party, including bobbing for apples and a haunted house. We joked that we didn't really need to do anything to make the house haunted. We could just let the big spiders stay on the walls instead of knocking them down with a broom and the cucarachas that jiggled the peanut butter lid over the shower drain could be our ghosts. We also had a water pipe outside the house that kept breaking, causing a geyser to shoot up unexpectedly from underground.

The morning of the Halloween party I borrowed a car to take LeRoy in for her operation. In the afternoon I picked the kids up from school and we went back to the vet's to bring LeRoy home.

LeRoy was not a pretty sight. She was weak and groggy and sore as she came out of the anesthetic. We put her in a little cardboard box to carry her. I assured Sharon and Lupe that after a while LeRoy would be just fine. On the way home Sharon leaned over the box to talk to LeRoy and stroke her.

When we got home, I carried the box with the cat into an unused bedroom and set the box on the empty bed. The window was open, but not very wide. We shut the door to the bedroom and left LeRoy inside, checking on her a few times as we got dressed for the party.

My friend Tammy, who was going to spend the night, came to the party early and helped with our makeup. The full impact of Sharon's old lady costume was realized as I watched Tammy draw lines and creases and wrinkles on Sharon's round freckled face. It was shocking to see the transformation of a little girl into a sad-looking little old lady.

Tammy and I had a lot more to do to get ready and the sun was setting. In La Paz there are breath-taking sunsets and that night was no exception. The sky became streaked with many different hues from bright orange to rosy pink as the adults started to arrive with their arms full of pots of food and bowls of salad and bottles of rum and tequila and mixers. We spread everything out on the table in the dining room and fixed ourselves a drink.

The apple bobbing would take place in the *lavadero*, the cement structure out in the yard where Huera, our part-time helper, washed our clothes by hand. Someone needed to fill it with water. We sent Doug, who was dressed as a sultan and wore a silk shirt and white pants and an aqua satin turban on his head, to do it.

Newly-arriving guests admired the decorations, especially the spider the size of a frying pan that was above the doorway. Nobody dared to challenge me when I said it was real. We finished decorating inside and lit the many candles around the house. The music was blaring from the radio in the back room.

The sky was dark and purple as the group of Mexican children arrived. Sharon ran outside to greet them. She took one little girl's hand and led her into the kitchen and the rest of them followed. No one noticed that their dogs had followed them into the yard.

They were shy at first, perhaps uncomfortable being in the presence of so many gringos. Some of the littler ones were scared of our costumes, especially of me because I was the Devil. We poured them soft drinks and directed them to the hors d'oeuvres. The adults admired their costumes and gradually they started to relax.

Soon they were running around inside and outside of the house, squealing happily. Boys were playing stick with Huckleberry in the front yard. The adults fixed themselves more drinks and I was thinking that it was just about time to start the games.

Suddenly there was screaming and snarling and yelling from outside. We heard a torrent of bad words and more unearthly high-pitched screaming. Had someone gotten hurt? The next minute Sharon came running into the kitchen crying, her face contorted, her old lady glasses askew. The lines on her face were twisted and etched even deeper. She was screaming something about LeRoy.

I ran for the bedroom and saw that the door was ajar. Other adults ran out into the yard. The cat was not in her box. I ran outside.

The whole group of Mexican kids were screaming and crying. Some of the boys were picking up rocks and throwing them at the dogs. "*Váyase, váyese,*" they yelled. "*Váyase.*" The dogs slunk away, but it was too late.

We found the cat lying not far from the house, mangled and bleeding and almost dead. The group of adults and kids stood around helplessly. I hugged Sharon and Lupe to me and tried to pull them away.

I led Sharon back to the kitchen. She was sobbing uncontrollably. There was nothing I could say. We sat down by the table and I rocked my little old lady back and forth. Her grief-stricken face tore me up.

People were milling around, fixing themselves drinks and walking around the house like zombies. Tammy fixed me a strong drink and brought it to me. One by one the Mexican children filed into the kitchen, standing around awkwardly as Sharon cried her heart out.

Lupe stood next to Sharon and patted her hand. Not wanting to see her sister so sad she said, "It's O.K. Sharon, we can get another cat." This sent Sharon into another paroxysm of crying.

After several minutes I asked Sharon if she wanted me to cancel the party. Her body still jerked with sobs, but she said, "No, let's have the party."

I dried her tears the best I could and we went on with the party. I told Doug, the one in the sultan costume, to pick up the dead cat and put her in one of Memo's nightgowns, then deposit it far away from the house under a tree. He nodded and walked stiffly outside.

When he came back he had blood on his white pants. He told me that the dogs had ripped open LeRoy's incision and that LeRoy had bled to death.

I don't remember much of the party. I never drank as much rum and Vita as I drank that night. Tammy and I stayed up after all the guests had gone and she helped me put the kids to bed. When I put Sharon's P.J.'s on and washed the makeup off her face, I wondered if she would ever be a little girl again.

Later Tammy and I drank some more and talked about what had happened. There was so much confusion at the time. I thought that one of the kids had opened the bedroom door and a dog had wandered into the room, that LeRoy had freaked out and mustered up the strength to jump out of the window, but was too groggy to run away from the dogs in the yard. They must have grabbed LeRoy and begun mauling her and that's when the children started yelling and screaming.

Tammy said she thought that LeRoy went out the window on her own accord, but didn't realize the dogs were out there and being so weak, she couldn't get away. Smelling blood, they tore after her.

The next day we were confronted with the horrible mess from the party and hangovers and what to do with LeRoy. My friend Tammy and I sat out on the hammock and tried to get mobilized. At that moment, Carlos, the man who had sold us Lupe's land, happened to be walking by on the beach. We called him over and asked him to dig a grave for the cat. He did it because he was somewhat smitten on my friend Tam. The dirt was hard as cement and it took him a long time.

While he dug the grave, Sharon and Lupe decorated a shoe box to put LeRoy in. They drew pictures of a cat with a halo and pictures of casas and trees and cucarachas on it. In her childish seven-year-old hand, Sharon wrote HERE LIES LEROY, SHE WAS A GOOD CAT on the side of the box.

When we were ready I directed Carlos to the spot where Doug had stashed LeRoy's body. Carlos put her in the box and brought it back to us. Sharon carried LeRoy to the gravesite. There were a lot more tears.

We had a little ceremony and buried LeRoy near the tree where she had been killed. The kids scattered flowers and put LeRoy's catnip mouse in the grave before we covered the box with dirt. We all said a few words.

Later in the day, some of the Mexican children came to the fence and stood around. We invited them in. Their dogs did not come with them.

LUPE'S LAND PART I

Right after Lupe was born we bought a piece of property in her name because eventually we wanted to move our sailboat rental and charter business down to La Paz. It was not a big piece, but it was waterfront property close to downtown. We felt lucky to score it.

Carlos Martinez, a relative of the couple that owned the land, set everything up, including finding a lawyer, who turned out to be a cousin of his. I recall that the minute they got the money the couple that we bought it from, split. The year was 1965 and the price was $1200.

When we bought the land it was in its natural semi-wild state. Shortly afterwards Cass and a friend called Peeky Douglas acquired four or five thirty-foot-long war canoes that were used in the shooting of the movie "Mutiny on the Bounty" and beached them on the property.

Making the canoes into sightseeing boats was part of the general plan for making a killing in Mexico. The boats would be powered by small diesel engines and would sport red and white striped canopies to protect balding and gray-haired tourists from the sun.

The boats would putt about the harbor during the day, ending up at Mogote, the peninsula across the bay, in the evening, where Mariachi players would emerge from the mangroves. There would be music, drinks and a barbeque for the appreciative guests.

We often sat on the back deck of the "Black Douglas" discussing future lucrative business deals while a fiery sunset lit up the skies. The more cocktails we drank, the faster the ideas came. There was nothing much like that happening there—La Paz was virgin territory. In retrospect, the ideas were not that crazy, just some years ahead of their time.

Before heading home that year we put a fence around the property consisting of some rickety *palos* and two strands of barbed wire and planted two little *piño* trees in either corner of the land.

The next year when we came down, Peeky Douglas had taken his boat back up to the States and he and his wife were separated. The war canoes were still there, but in sad shape. We let the Mexican boys take them out and paddle around, and then we lost track of them.

A few years later we were still planning to move our sailboat charter business to Lupe's land when someone informed us that the government owned the first 10 meters of beach back from the high water mark. Since this would cut into the land considerably, we needed to do something.

Cass had one of his brilliant ideas. He heard that they were tearing down a building downtown so he lined up the kids in the neighborhood to help him build a breakwater. He paid off the job foreman to divert dump trucks full of brick and stone and debris down to Lupe's land to build a breakwater in order to fill in the beach.

Soon there was a parade of trucks going back and forth to the land and a brigade of kids carrying the stones out to Cass who stood in the water with a cigar in his mouth placing the rocks in position. Sharon and Lupe, who was now a toddler, and the littlest Mexican kids helped fill in the gaps with smaller rocks. The scene was reminiscent of the building of the pyramids.

I watched for a while, but then left with the baby, Memo, to feed him and then both of us would take a nap at the house that we had rented several blocks away.

The project was well underway when the *policía* arrived to call a halt. Cass pleaded "*no comprende*" when they told him to stop because what he was doing was illegal. To stall for time, Cass brought the officers to the house to have his *esposa*, namely me, interpret for him. In the meantime, the parade of dump trucks continued.

I was irritated with Cass for waking me up and bringing the police to the house. I knew that he understood what they were saying all along. But by the time I translated their message to him, the job was done and Lupe's land was preserved. (It wasn't only in Mexico that Cass operated outside of the law. I was always having to try to cover up for what he did.)

We didn't move the boat rental business to La Paz as originally planned; we sold it instead. Then about five years later we got a divorce and I went on a raft trip across the Atlantic Ocean.

Going our separate ways, we lost touch with Lupe's land. I moved off the boat into an apartment and was busy trying to support myself and three kids as a waitress. Cass bought a fish boat and had his own problems with the IRS and the FBI. For several years neither of us paid the taxes on the land, even though they were only $4 a year the last time we paid them.

When Lupe was about 10 years old, we got word from Mary Shroyer that there was a rumor going around that Carlos had resold Lupe's land. There was not much we could do from up here. We didn't know any Mexican lawyers and didn't have the money to find one. Our friends in La Paz who looked into the matter for us all seemed to think it was hopeless. Cass wanted to go down and "kill that son of a bitch, Carlos."

In the years that followed each of us made occasional short visits to La Paz, and when we did, the land was just as we left it-the crooked weathered fence posts with the two strands of barbed wire around them, the beach filling in from the prevailing winds, and the two *piño* trees we had planted growing rapidly. We had given up hope of ever getting the property back, but we still called it "Lupe's land."

Another 10 years went by. Then in 1991 I went back to La Paz with my friend, Tammy, for a vacation and for some reason at the last minute I stuffed all the papers having to do with the land in my suitcase.

The afternoon before we were to fly home, we were sitting having a drink with the Shroyers in the restaurant at their marina. Their eldest son, Neil, who had been a kid every other time we had been there, had since graduated from college at Humboldt State and was working in the family business. Suddenly he brought up the subject of Lupe's land.

"What are you going to do about Lupe's land?" he wanted to know. "You should try to get it back." (I think he had a crush on Lupe when she was down there as a teenager). Then Neil mentioned that he had a Mexican friend who was a lawyer. He wondered if we had a bill of sale or any other papers.

I told him that I just happened to have all the papers with me and by all means he could show them to his friend. It was one of those great moments when the planets were in direct alignment.

After leaving all the papers and the bill of sale with Neil, Tammy and I took a cab to the airport. When I got home I reported to the family members what had happened, but warned them not to get their hopes up.

When we heard back from Neil's lawyer friend he said that we had a good chance of getting the land back because Carlos had not put the proper notification in the newspaper when he claimed that we had abandoned it.

That's when we picked up the cry of "Lupe's Land" again. It inspired us like "El Grito de Dolores" or "Remember the Alamo," and we would rally around it for years.

Our lawyer in La Paz filed a civil suit to nullify the illegal sale, and Neil advised us to "move something onto the land quickly" before the other guy did.

The warm weather and relaxed atmosphere of Mexico appealed to Cass after a cold wet winter on the boat in Sausalito. So we chipped in and bought him a secondhand trailer which he stocked full of canned goods, dog food, Green Death (Rainier ale), and cigars. Then he hitched the trailer to the back of his old yellow pickup and he and his dog headed south...to squat on Lupe's Land.

ROXANA

When I first met Roxana she was about four years old. I was standing outside of Lupe's land, trying to get the rusty lock on the gate open so that I could get inside and check out the trailer.

"*Chingada a tu madre!*" I swore as I jerked at the frozen lock. I was about to give up when I looked up and saw a little girl watching me. She quickly ran away. I thought my cussing had scared her.

A few minutes later to my surprise, the little girl reappeared with a can of W-D 40. She held it out to me and then backed up, shy and skittish-like. I thanked her and after squirting the lock several times, it popped open.

Grateful for her help, I invited the little girl in. She was reluctant about following me until I told her that I was going to "*limpia la casa.*" Then she came timidly through the gate. I asked her what her name was and she whispered "Roxana."

When Roxana and I stepped inside the trailer, we found a mess. Because of his sudden departure, my ex-husband had left dirty pots in the sink, and books and papers on the table. A layer of dust, thick as snow, lay over everything. I berated myself for getting involved with Lupe's land and the trailer.

The trailer had suffered from the long haul to La Paz and then after Cass was arrested for trespassing, it had been sitting unattended for several months.

I handed Roxana the broom while I removed the mattresses, the cushions, and the bedding and took them outside for a beating. I went back inside to start cleaning the table and the pots and pans and the stove. Roxana was sweeping with a fury, like one possessed. When she was done inside the trailer, she hopped outside and began furiously sweeping the ground in front of the door. Great clouds of dust and dirt blew back in my face and back into the trailer.

I relieved her of the broom and sent Roxana to pick up the garbage in the yard instead. I pulled out large green plastic garbage bags and showed her how to do it.

After we finished she looked at me like what are we going to do next, so I invited her back inside the trailer. I pulled out some paper and pencil and had her draw some pictures. She drew little houses, palm trees, and dogs and cats, while I snuck peeks at her and attempted to sketch her face.

Roxana had expressive almond-shaped eyes, dark eyebrows and long lashes, pierced ears with tiny earrings, and a bow-shaped mouth. Her skin was a nice shade of brown. I was engrossed in shading in her beautiful face with the side of my pencil when I noticed Roxana frowning at what I was doing. She leaned over and erased the shading on her face.

When we were done drawing, I got my tennis racket and a couple of balls out of my backpack and took her outside. I put the racket in her hand and because she was so little, she needed two hands to hold it up. I tossed tennis balls at her and every time one of them would bounce off the racket strings she would double over with laughter. I took some photos of us.

That night when I left the trailer for my cheap hotel she skipped along beside me. In front of her house she stopped and waved at me until I was out of sight. The next day I invited her in again. After that Roxana didn't need an invitation to come inside the gate.

During our times together I had a bit of trouble understanding Roxana because she spoke Spanish very fast and in such a subdued voice. Nevertheless, I found out that her father was a fisherman and the brother of Carlos, the guy who had sold us the land and then resold it out from under us. Her mother was the grey-haired woman with most of her front teeth missing who watched me from the doorway of their house—the woman I thought was her grandmother. The little boy that played on the front stoop was not her brother; Roxana was his aunt.

I spent a week in La Paz that spring when I first met Roxana. When I went back to California, I promised to write to Roxana and send copies of the photos I had taken. When I did I made sure not to send ones that made her skin look too dark.

When I returned to La Paz the following year, I brought a box of second-hand clothing, a couple of old metal tennis rackets, a deck of cards, some coloring books and crayons, and a hand-held tape recorder.

After we cleaned the trailer and the land, I got Roxana to record some songs for me. At first she sang in a very small voice and when

I played them back she was terribly embarrassed. But when she heard my lame rendition of *"El Rancho Grande,"* she loosened up and began belting out her numbers. She sang with lots of emotion and with vibrato—more like a professional singer than a child of four.

Every afternoon I would walk down to the trailer and Roxana and I would spend more time together, coloring, singing into the tape recorder, and playing Old Maid or jacks.

Our relationship came to have a certain pattern and ritual about it. When I would walk toward Lupe's land, Roxana would come flying out of her house or run from the beach to greet me. If Roxana's mother was the one who saw me first, she would yell, *"Roxannaaaaa...la gringa!"* and Roxana would come running out of someone else's *casa*.

Being called "la gringa" was something which I didn't particularly like. Once I tried to get Roxana to call me by my real name. *"No llamame la gringa, por favor. Me llamo Maria,"* I said solemnly. Every time after that, she called me *"La Gringa Maria,"* and I let it go at that.

"Gringa Maria, vamos a limpiar!" Roxana would announce.

First we would clean the inside of the trailer and Roxana would sweep. Then Roxana would go down to the beach and fill a few pots with water so that I could wipe down the table and the stove and the sink. After that we would go outside with the green plastic garbage bags and pick up the garbage that was strewn anew all over the land.

"Vamos a colorear!" she would say when we finished. I would take out the crayons and the marking pens and the coloring books and the paper. In the coloring books, Roxana made the people's skin pink, their eyes blue, and their hair yellow. I would tack the new drawings up next to the earlier ones on the cupboards and on the closet door.

If we were hungry we would walk to the store a few blocks away and buy ourselves a soft drink and some chips. Other kids in the neighborhood who had previously been watching us, began following us. They started to hang on the fence hoping to be invited in.

Cass had never let any of the kids come inside the fence, although he scattered rice near the trailer for the chickens and let them wander in and out freely. He would dole out bits of Hershey chocolate through the fence—one tiny square to each kid and wait for them to say *gracias*.

I was never able to set up boundaries like that, but Roxana could. She would be the one to decide who would be allowed inside. Of those, only a few would be allowed to color. I was careful not to pay too much attention to the other kids because if I did, Roxana would get mad.

One of the activities we engaged in that included all the kids was to take the tennis rackets and the balls to the beach across the road and play a wild form of "baseball tennis."

In addition to being a little jealous of me, Roxana was extremely competitive and if things did not go her way she would fold her arms over her chest, narrow her eyes, and walk away. I would have to go over and put my arm around her and coax her back. I would make some joke and see the smile play around the corners of her lips and know that all was forgiven.

Sometimes when the pressure of entertaining became too much, I would try to sneak by Roxana's house without anyone seeing me, and would try to open the lock and remove the chain around the gate without having it rattle. I would pull the curtains so they wouldn't see me, and then I could read a book or write in peace. The only other way I could get some time alone was to tell Roxana that I needed to take a "*siesta*" something like "*limpia la casa*" that she could relate to.

During the eight years that we waited for the judge to decide who owned the land, I made two or three pilgrimages a year to check on Lupe's land, and each time Roxana was waiting for me. I have many memories from our times together, but one of the most striking is the recollection of what she said to me one day when she was about nine years old.

We were hanging out and I had asked her the question that adults always seem to pose to young children. "*Qué quieres hacerte, Roxana?*" (What do you want to be when you grow up?)

She thought for just a few seconds and replied, "*Una gringa.*

LA NOCHE BUENA

I heard Amada whisper, "Dale a Maria," and I cringed with fear. Dear God, please no, don't pass the doll to me. It was midnight on Christmas Eve, 1996. I envied the men who were still hanging out in the back of the house drinking. It seemed that only women and children were required to kiss and welcome the little ceramic Jesus figure that was being passed around the circle. I was a big awkward gringa woman, not a religious person, and baby Jesus was coming to me.

I had received an invitation earlier that week to spend "La Noche Buena" with the Mexican family of Amada and Alvaro and their four children. Being bilingual, at about a grade school level conversationally, I was envied by other gringos who could not share the experiences I had in another culture. However, I accepted the invitation before I found out that my sister had been killed in a car accident.

"Horrible, horrible" my mother had written in her fax. I was stunned by the news and anxious to go back and join my family, but there was nothing I could do because I couldn't get a flight out until Christmas Day. Because I didn't want to be alone on Christmas Eve in my tiny cold hotel room with its blue painted walls, I went to Alvaro and Amada's house as planned.

Amada said to come about seven, which seemed a late hour for me and for the twins who were just babies. I left the hotel just as it was getting dark and walked, hoping that we would eat soon and I would be back home early.

When I arrived, I was surprised that absolutely no preparations were being made for dinner—no pots on the stove, no cooking smells, no table set, nobody dressed. Amada said that the twins were napping. Sarai, about eight years old, was watching television. Alvaro, the man of the house, was not home from work yet.

Alvaro worked two jobs—during the day for a government agency and three nights a week as a teacher at a technical school. Amada, despite the fact that she had four children and two of them were the 6 month old twins, Danielle and Daniella, worked on the weekends at an orphanage, two all night shifts and three days.

Amada greeted me warmly and asked me how I was. I told her that my sister had been killed in a car accident the day before. She was sympathetic, but did not seem overly shocked. I found out later that she had 11 siblings, and three were already dead. Amada offered me tequila but I knew that my Spanish would turn to gibberish if I had anything to drink on an empty stomach. I also feared that I might fall off the chair and dissolve in a puddle of emotions.

What to do with me? Maybe I should walk back to the hotel and come back later. But no, Alvaro Jr. the 12-year-old son, brought out a deck of cards and sat me down at the kitchen table to play. He and his sister, Sarai, alternated from being clownish and smiling to being pensive and sullen-looking. Fortunately, we had a deck of cards and games in common with which to bridge the gap between us.

I was heartened when a half hour later Amada came in the kitchen with a bag of groceries. She lit the gas stove with a match and got out a huge pot, then began cutting up meat and vegetables and putting them in the pot.

Amada wiped strands of wet black hair off her forehead as she cooked and carried on a conversation. She also managed to watch us play cards out of the corner of her eye and smoke. She lit a cigarette, twisting her head away from the pot to take a drag on it so as not to get ashes in our dinner. I was able to understand most of what she said in Spanish and respond to it, but not all of it. From time to time she would stop stirring and put a finger to her lips to listen for the twins.

When they finally woke up she went in and changed their diapers, and brought them into the kitchen. She sat them in their little infant seats on the floor, and resumed chatting, smoking, and stirring the big pot on the stove.

In the meantime, Alvaro Sr. arrived home, and Amada called Sarai to get dressed and quit watching the TV. Alvaro Jr. gathered up the playing cards and went to change. When he and Sarai returned they were wearing new fleecy pastel sweat suits that Amada had sewn for them. Sarai came into the kitchen to entertain both me and the twins who sat wide-eyed and innocent, waiting and wondering what was going to happen next.

It turned out that we were not going to stay there, we were going to "Papi's" (Amada's father's house) for "La Noche Buena." When everyone was ready we filed outside and piled into a taxi. Alvaro sat with one of the twins in the front seat, and the rest of us scrunched into the back seat with the large kettle of stew on the floor of the car between our feet.

Traffic was a mess. Everyone seemed to be going somewhere that night. Dust and people swirled before us in the headlights like snowflakes in a snowstorm. The driver laid on the horn as the car meandered lawlessly from one side of the road to the other. We were jostled back and forth in the back seat, but miraculously no one got hot stew spilled on their feet.

When we pulled up in front of Amada's parents' house, kids were paying soccer and tag in the street. The place was alive with people. Other family members were climbing out of cars and vans. We got out of the taxi and everyone kissed and hugged everyone else. Amada grabbed my hand and introduced me to each person who also hugged me as if I were also part of the family, although I knew that I was the lanky old *gringa* woman.

Next I was led into the living room where I was introduced to more sisters and aunts and nieces and brothers-in-law and cousins, and hugged again. The names were all a blur, I gave up on trying to remember who everybody was, getting only a rough idea of their relationship to Amada and the size of this family.

Looking around I saw a small decorated tree, about four feet tall, with twinkling lights in the corner of the room. There were a few gifts underneath the tree and an impressive nativity scene, although the crib where the baby Jesus was supposed to be was empty.

The prominence of the nativity scene under the tree did not surprise me. Everywhere one went in La Paz at this time of year there was a nativity scene—at the supermarket, at the bank, at the airport, on the road from the airport, in the lobby of my hotel, in front yards, even at the beach. Everywhere one was reminded that this was a religious holiday.

Introductions being over in the living room, I was led through the kitchen, where I met more women, and then followed Alvaro to the cemented back patio where all the men were sitting or standing with drinks and cigarettes in their hands and laughing and talking. I was introduced all around. Several men jumped up to give me their seat.

They sat me down in a plastic chair and asked me if I wanted a *cerveza*. Since I was about to faint from hunger, anything that had calories in it was fine with me, and a beer was delivered to me by one of the women.

I took several sips and then set the beer down. I did not want to give the false impression that I was a drunken *gringa*. I noticed that the women, if they ventured out to the patio, did not stay long and they drank less freely. They were all busy in the kitchen or busy taking care of the younger children.

The beer helped me feel less awkward and when asked about my connection to La Paz, I told them, in my halting Spanish, of arriving in a sailboat in 1964 and about the birth of two of my children in La Paz. Then, as my tongue loosened, I digressed into the time that I drifted across the Atlantic Ocean on a raft and left my children and my husband at home. I noticed the men giving each other dubious looks and the questioning of me tapered off. This was too wild a tale for them to accept from a woman, even a *gringa* woman.

I was relieved to be out of the spotlight. The conversation turned to soccer and then someone spoke of witnessing a car accident which set me thinking about my sister again. They were laughing at the image of the car spinning around out of control and the drunken driver getting out and complaining that the car he had hit had hit him. I accepted another *cerveza* and wandered into the living room.

Alvaro Jr. came in dripping with sweat and asked Amada if he could take his top off but she didn't want him in just his bare skin. I went outside to watch the kids play and indecorously kicked a few balls myself. When Amada came outside to round up the children, I thought it must finally be time to eat. It was already about 11:30.

"*Ven, Maria,*" she said as she took my hand and led me in as if I was also a child.

We were to be part of some ceremony in the living room in front of the tree. The women arranged us in a circle and had everybody hold hands. There were no men in the room, only women and children including boys up to puberty, and me. The mood changed from jocular to serious as a woman picked up a Bible and began reading in a very strong voice. She read a passage from Luke about Mary and Joseph being able to find lodging that night. In her other hand the woman reading held a small china doll figure of the infant Jesus.

Completing the reading with the birth of baby Jesus, the woman put the Bible down. She made the sign of the cross and fussed over the tiny doll. With an adoring look on her face she kissed it, and then passed it on to the woman next to her who did the same. One by one the women and children in the circle rocked the doll, talked to it and kissed it before passing it on to the next person. I was planning how I could slink away when I heard Amada tell Sarai to give it to me. The women's faces were beaming and smiling and watching me as Sarai passed Jesus to me.

My worst fear was that I would be clumsy and drop the doll, shattering their Christmas much as my own Christmas had been shattered by the death of my sister. But, miraculously, I didn't. First I rocked the doll, which I noticed was light as to be almost weightless and so quiet and peaceful, unlike any babies I had known. Then I kissed the doll and murmured something in English like "I hope you have a long and happy life," which seemed to please everyone and I passed the doll on. I might have even made the sign of the cross. I have been known to do anything for food, even being hypocritical.

The food was set out just after midnight. The men came back in to join us. We got our plates, helping ourselves to a variety of dishes, mashed potatoes, salad, and the barbecued turkey dish of Amada's. There were not enough places to sit and many stood around balancing their plates in one hand as they ate, but I was given a seat of honor on the sofa.

The taste, odor, and consistency of the food was unlike anything I had eaten before. Even the mashed potatoes, were foreign to me and, starved as I was, I ate tentatively. My thoughts drifted to being at my mother's house in Wisconsin on Christmas Eve. We ate oyster stew, and lutefisk and lefse, rolling the lutefisk (codfish), up in the soft tortilla-shaped potato and lard-based lefse. We kids turned up our noses at the fish, just putting mounds of butter and sugar on our lefse, rolling it up and devouring it that way.

I wondered if at my mother's house they were still carrying on that tradition on this Christmas Eve that had so much sadness and death in it. I wondered also what a Mexican visitor to my mother's house would think of our food and our customs. Would they assume that the thing that looked like a tortilla would taste like a tortilla, like I expected the mashed potatoes would be familiar to me?

During the cleanup, the men disappeared again, back out on the patio to drink or out in the street, and the children ran outside again. I was amazed that the dozens of children were still running around and going strong. I admired their stamina, (just as my daughter had admired the Mexicans being able to eat the little Jalapeno pepper that I watched her bite into and spit out on an airplane once).

Sitting quietly, I was wondering when we would do presents so I could go home and crawl back into my hotel room and go to sleep. I was beginning to ache from exhaustion and from dealing with so much grief earlier in the day.

I looked at the tree and could not believe that there would be enough presents for all the children that were now being herded in the door. Oh, but it was a happy time. Each child got exactly one gift. The boys got a gun or toy car, the girls got a doll, or a tea set. No fancy computer games, expensive roller blades, game boys, or remote control cars, they got simple things, like the Guatemalan doll in traditional dress that Sarai received.

She smiled happily as she examined the bright pink and red stripped skirt and smoothed the yarn hair on the doll's head. I asked to see it. "*Como se llama a tu muneca?*" I asked her. She looked at the doll for a minute and then answered, "*Mari, se llama Mari. Como tu.*" I was honored that she would name her doll after me and I wasn't sure that I deserved it.

After the presents were opened it was time for dessert. A sheet cake, an ornate pastel with white frosting from the store, was brought in. It was cut into tiny squares and set on the table in the dining room for those who were interested, along with cups of jello.

After dessert and after playing with and admiring the toy that each child got, the adults started to collect their pots and pans and sweaters and jackets and children. The hugging and well-wishing that occurred when we arrived was repeated upon departure. "*Feliz navidad, feliz navidad*," was spoken over and over again and everyone embraced everyone else.

As we stumbled outside the taxi was magically waiting for us. I noticed that inside a few of the vans parked outside, the younger men were carrying on their drinking party.

On the drive home, the twins fell asleep. Even talkative Amada was subdued. Alvaro directed the taxi driver to my hotel. It was an unusual place for a *gringa* woman to be staying. Alvaro said that he and Amada had stayed there a few nights when they were waiting to move into a different house.

Sarai was sitting next to me in the back seat and as we drove along she suddenly thrust her doll at me to hold. I tried to give it back to her when we pulled up in front of the hotel, but she shook her head and put it back in my hands. "*Para ti*," she insisted. I couldn't believe it. This eight-year-old girl was giving me her one Christmas present.

I climbed out of the car and they drove off. Then I realized how late it was. The heavy wooden fortress-like doors to my hotel were locked up tight. I pounded on the doors and yelled, "*Abre la puerta, ábrela*," until I was hoarse and nearly hysterical.

The grief of my sister's death, the strangeness of the evening, and now being locked out of my inn, hit me all at once. I sat down on the curb and sobbed, my emotions spilling out. I cursed life and the world. After about a half hour I pulled myself together and approached the wall again, still cursing and yelling for someone to open up. I hoisted myself up to try and scale it. I threw the doll over the wall and fell back down to the sidewalk, feeling abandoned and rejected.

My yelling was not heard, but my sobbing was. Magically the doors opened. I retrieved my doll and marched with some dignity past the sleepy hotel employee. I went to my tiny blue cell of a room and went to bed.

ACALI

It was just before dawn, about 5:30 a.m., although time meant little to us who had been drifting on the ocean for nearly 100 days.

Santiago and José Maria, the Argentinian man, had the four a.m. to eight watch that morning, and they saw the red and green lights of the freighter getting closer and closer long before they woke up Maria or any of the rest of us.

It was the time of day when the black starlit night changed to shades of gray and the sun would rise up out of the water to bring us another hot day and very little wind.

The raft was named Acali, an Aztec word for "House On Water," although in the media we were called the "Raft of Passion." The truth was that in the heat of the Caribbean we avoided contact with one another's body and competed for any bit of shade or air.

I could hear them talking, a murmur of male voices. They were probably discussing their research as the Argentinian was Santiago's assistant and his student.

Our raft with its international crew was supposed to be all about women's lib with the women in the key positions of captain, navigator, doctor, scientist, and the men as cook, photographer, or priest. Santiago, leader of the expedition, was supposed to be taking orders from Maria, our Swedish captain, when it came to matters concerning the sea, but there was bad blood between them. I was the navigator.

The final straw came one day when Santiago asked us to write down what we liked about our home on water and what we didn't like. What Maria wrote was brutally honest. "I hate the raft. It is not a boat. It is impossible to maneuver. That's why I hate it."

Santiago could not tolerate the captain of his vessel making a statement like that. So after we had drifted past Barbados and were well into the Caribbean, Santiago called a meeting. He informed us Maria was no longer captain. From then on he would give the orders.

Maria accepted his decree without a protest. We who were loyal to her were disappointed when she merely got up and left the cabin. She sat by herself on deck looking off into the distance. I told her that no matter what Santiago said, she was still captain to me. She shrugged and remained silent.

I was closer to Maria because she and I worked together with our sextants to get our noon position. Also because Maria had smuggled half a dozen bottles of Scotch aboard which she shared with just a chosen few.

Before dawn on the morning of the freighter, Maria was sleeping heavily, probably due to the fact that she was drinking more Scotch after losing her command.

Light was just seeping into the area inside of the plywood structure that we called a cabin. It was like so many other similar dawns on the raft—a slight rolling, the shafts of light, the dreams of coffee or of sex, the limbs of our bodies flung outside of our light nylon sleeping bags, hair strewn across our sweaty faces, the men with beards and rough faces. Charles was snoring next to me and Fé was moaning. Eisuke was talking in his sleep in Japanese.

I heard the Argentinian come into the cabin, and saw him step over the forms of bodies and half-conscious faces until he reached the form of Maria and shook her shoulder. "Maria, wake up."

I saw Maria look at him with one quizzical eye open and the other still shut. "Why do you need me when Santiago is with you on your watch," she asked with a touch of bitterness in her voice.

"Please, Maria." He stood over her staring with his serious eyes until finally she got up slowly and pulled on her shorts and muttered something in Swedish. I was fully awake by now, but chose to bury my head in my arms, rather than getting up to see what was going on.

I heard angry words from outside and a few minutes later, Maria returned and yelled for Fé, our radioperson who was the other American and a black woman, to wake up. "Get on the radio," Maria said.

Fé who took sleeping pills at night said, "Huh," and opened and closed her eyes a few times before she became awake and crawled over a few bodies to get to the marine radio. Maria also yelled at me to get up.

I went out on deck and faced the reality of a ship bearing down on us. After so many days of seeing nothing but water in every direction, there it was. The red and green lights were lined up in a configuration that my training and experiences at sea with my husband told me was trouble.

Cass had always instructed me to wake him up if I had any doubts about whether a vessel was headed for us or headed away from us, or would pass us by to the port or to the starboard.

The raft, like our boats, had a radar reflector, an oddly-shaped piece of tin up the mast that was supposed to be picked up by a ship's radar, although I didn't have much confidence in it.

Cass's words went through my head. "Even if there was anyone looking at the screen, and often there is no one there, and no one on the bridge or on the deck of those big mothers…even if they saw something they wouldn't change course. Hell no, would cost them too much money," he said.

All of these thoughts went through my head as I looked at the enormous hulk of the ship getting close and closer. Even if they miss us, if we aren't far enough away, we will be sucked up in their wake and dragged under and drowned.

Maria, after her initial anger at Santiago for waiting so long to wake her up, was quite clam as she issued orders. "Mary, get out the flares. Eisuke, get the life boats ready." I scrambled back into the cabin and pawed at the floorboards. I knew exactly which bin they were stored in, all wrapped in several layers of thick plastic and taped together.

Fé was still on the radio with her headset on, her eyes rolling around like marbles. She just kept shaking her head as she tried to raise the ship. She tried every frequency on the dial and was greeted with static or a faint far-off voice of some fishermen, but they didn't acknowledge her either. Finally, she resorted to "May day, may day," and began broadcasting our position.

My fingers trembled as I tore off the black electrical tape and unwrapped the precious flares. I had never even had to light the ones that were in the glove compartment of my car, and I wasn't sure how to do it. I grabbed a box of matches and hunched over to clear the cabin doorway and go back on deck.

When I returned with the flares it was still there, bigger than life. The rest of the crew were waving their arms wildly and whistling and screaming in hopes that someone on the freighter would see us. Santiago had picked up a bullhorn that we didn't even know he had and was yelling to get their attention.

It was light by this time. We could see the pilot house of the ship and we could see the upper and lower deck, but there was not one person in sight. The ship, nonetheless, moved steadily ahead on automatic.

I lit off a flare. It rocketed skyward, burning brightly and brilliantly for a few seconds, then stopped in its tracks and fizzling, came tumbling down and fell in a useless heap into the ocean. From the gigantic ship we got no response. Maria yelled at me to keep lighting the flares off. For some strange reason I was afraid of using them all up, but I lit off another and another.

As the ship came bearing down toward us there was a fascination and horror, and an unreal quality to our situation. O.K. you can stop now. We've had enough of this joke, I wanted to say, as I saw death bearing down on us.

There was no way to avoid the "accident" that would kill us all, and it was happening in slow motion. This was not going to be quick like the sudden darting of a car across a divider that you haven't had time to see coming.

I continued to light off flares, that was my job, and I stopped looking up to see if they had been acknowledged. Fé stuck her head out of the cabin and ducked her head back in again. "They are not picking us up," she said over her shoulder.

There were only two flares left when Maria said, "I think they are turning. Yes, they are changing course."

The bow of the ship slowly angled away from us. It seemed a mighty effort for it to change direction. Instead of a head-on view, we now could see the side of the freighter as it continued on toward us. I set off another flare to make sure they saw us.

Aboard the raft, we laughed and hugged each other. Even those among us who were no longer friends clung to each other appreciatively.

Bernardo, our black Catholic priest from Angola, smiled serenely as he had done every day of the voyage.

When the ship came very close to us we could see the figure of someone on deck. Santiago took up his bullhorn again and aimed it at them. Standing up by the tiller, looking like a little Napoleon, he screamed, "Who is in command there? Why don't you watch where you're going!"

Maria shook her head, went back to bed, and we went back to drifting.

MERKABA MAN

Whenever I went to La Paz I could never predict what my experiences would be. As a poor gringa, I didn't stay in starred hotels, frequent fancy restaurants, or rent cars. I stayed in the trailer on Lupe's land, in the back of somebody's house, at El Convento, (the cheapest hotel in La Paz), or on a boat. To get anywhere, I mainly walked.

One day, at a time when I was feeling that life was dull, I got a fax. It was an invitation to join a friend in La Paz who had bought a boat and was fixing it up in preparation for sailing it north to San Francisco Bay. I jumped at the chance, even though I didn't particularly like Phillip, the owner of the boat. I expected to help him out a little in exchange for a place to stay.

It was a sweltering hot day in April when I arrived. Because Phillip was in such a rush to bring the boat north, its insides and outsides were all torn up. There was no water, no head, the refrigeration wasn't working, and the sink was full of tools. There was only one shore boat and Phillip needed it to be at his disposal.

The boat was anchored way out across the bay, next to the uninhabited shores of El Mogote, a mangrove and bug-infested peninsula where sting rays lurked beneath the water. There was no place to hide from the brutal sun as the boat swung around on its tether. I had a free place to stay, but there was plenty wrong with the arrangement.

The worse part was the energy of Phillip. In his rush to get the boat north, he was encountering problem after problem, first a rusty fuel tank, next a leaking deck, then worn rigging. The boat had sat around the harbor for years. I started talking to myself. Some vacation! How did this happen? I was trapped. I picked up a piece of sandpaper and grudgingly went to work.

I was to sleep up in the fo'c'sle, while Phillip slept on the bunk in the main salon. At least I would not be woken at four in the morning when his alarm went off and he got up to meditate. His practice was to light some incense, and sit very still for two hours under a blanket and chant.

We went to bed early. I lay awake for some time looking up at the stars through the opened hatch, feeling a welcomed fresh breeze on my face, and stewed about my situation. Since Phillip was also a vegetarian and a herbal tea person, I could not even look forward to my morning coffee.

After three days of being on the boat, my fingertips were sandpapered raw and my hands reeked of paint thinner. As I worked, Phillip brought a steady stream of "experts" aboard the boat to give him advice. I felt like I was just the robotic deckhand sanding and painting away. At the end of each day Phillip was clever enough to compliment me on my work. "You have such a fine hand for painting. No one could do it any better," he would say.

The only real pleasure was going ashore to take a shower at the end of the day. Many years ago while working with my husband on our own boat I had discovered that the hotter, dirtier, and more tired you are, the better a shower feels. After a day of working with Phillip, the shower was ecstasy.

On the third night, upon returning from taking our showers, Phillip started cooking a large pot of his meatless spaghetti sauce. He mentioned that he'd invited a guest aboard. I was to make a big salad. He was going to take the shore boat to pick him up.

At first I resented Phillip bringing someone aboard. I was sure that he was inviting this person only in order to pump him for information, get some free advice, or maybe some help. That's the way Phillip was.

As I ripped up the lettuce and chopped the vegetables, my mood was not good. I reflected on how my husband used to bring unexpected guests on the boat all the time for me to cook for and how angry it would make me. Now that I was a single woman whose children were grown, I ate when and what I pleased at home.

I was thinking about jumping ship. I had about enough money with me to stay the last three or four nights of my vacation at El Convento, my cheap hotel, and eat at the fish taco stand downtown.

My brooding thoughts were interrupted when I heard the skiff bump against the side of the boat and heard Phillip say sharply, "Hold her off, will you. Don't bump the boat." I heard the guest apologize. Then there was a thumping of feet on the deck and in the cockpit. I moved the salad bowl off the steps of the companionway so they could come below.

Phillip stooped to enter the galley and main salon, as he was 6' 4" tall. The man that followed him was shorter and more solidly built. He tossed his duffle bag onto one of the upper bunks and turned around.

The man, who was probably in his 50's, had an interesting face. Old-fashioned round glasses gave him a slightly spacey look and enlarged his piercing blue eyes. There was a gap between his front teeth so that when he grinned he looked like a jack-o-lantern. He stretched out a blonde hairy arm to meet me.

His name was Michael. I had long since given up the notion of any romance entering my life, so the tingling sensation I got when I took his hand startled me. He grinned pleasantly. Phillip lit several candles and we sat down to dinner.

During the conversation I learned that Michael had a wealth of boating experience and was an expert in wiring, rigging, and engine repair. Originally from the Pacific Northwest, he now lived in Pescadero, a small town on the Pacific side of Baja near Todos Santos. He had a ranch with a doughboy pool on it. He intended to turn the ranch into a surf shop, but there was some kind of problem with a Mexican wife or ex-wife. Michael was willing to work for Phillip because he needed the money for his lawyer.

After dinner Michael entertained us with his stories. It seemed that he had had many close calls and near sinkings. I was interested, but I think Phillip thought that he was exaggerating or even lying. He kept trying unsuccessfully to steer the conversation back to the tasks at hand on the boat. Eventually Phillip grew tired and yawned, indicating that it was time for bed.

As we said goodnight, Michael asked Phillip if he had any coffee aboard. Phillip said, no, and Michael told him that he couldn't start work without a cup of coffee. Phillip hastily assured him that he would borrow some coffee from a neighboring boat so we could start work at seven.

"Just ask for the whole beans," said Michael. He pulled an old-fashioned coffee grinder and a coffee pot from his duffle bag.

"Bless you, Michael," I said to myself. I had an ally.

The next morning, as Phillip waited for Michael on deck, Michael showed me how to operate the old wooden grinder. "One has to take one's time," he said, and he put his hand on mine to slow down my turning of the crank. My heart sped up. I was physically attracted to him despite myself.

While Michael and Phillip discussed the day's projects, I savored the experience of grinding. I turned the crank slowly, in touch with every sensation. The aroma of fresh coffee that had been missing from my life for several days was overpowering. This was an exercise in meditation as surely as sitting under a blanket and chanting was.

When the coffee was ready, I called Michael down. Phillip surprised me by taking time out too to prepare himself a cup of tea. We ate some granola and then went to work on the boat.

During the rest of the day Michael and I had very little opportunity to talk because Phillip kept us both busy on opposite ends of the boat. All the most back-breaking, dirty, and dangerous jobs were Michael's. He winked at me once when he saw me stealing looks at him.

Michael wore shorts and his legs were muscular and shapely, like those of a much younger man. His legs were covered with the same tawny blonde hair as his arms were. When he moved it was gracefully and powerfully with a springy light step—like a big Cat.

We worked until sundown. At dinner I sat across from Michael. After dinner, we started talking about the coming millennium. The conversation was getting way out there, with Michael proposing that there would be a major pole shift at the end of the century. Life as we know it for most people and for the planet will end, he said. Phillip had had enough of our talk and got up to clear the plates.

"If you are interested, read this," said Michael. He reached inside his duffle bag and pulled out a slick paperback and laid it down on the table. On the shiny pink and green cover two slim blue-skinned creatures with large heads on top of long necks were walking this way. A Frisbee-shaped space vehicle hovered behind them. The title of the book was *Nothing in This Book Is True, But It's Exactly How Things Are.*

I picked the book up and Michael sat down beside me. He started to explain some of the ideas in the book, but I had a difficult time concentrating on what he was saying because our bare legs were touching under the table.

"Interesting title," was all that I could say.

Phillip finished the dishes and reminded us that we should be getting some sleep. We had a big day tomorrow. My legs were weak when I arose from the table.

"Take the book," Michael said. So I took it up into the fo'c'sle with me and turned on the little bunk light and started to read.

I was a math teacher in Marin and prided myself in being a logical thinker. All my life I had steered away from science fiction or astrology or anything that was a bit hokey. But here I was reading about earthlings being abducted periodically by a race of aliens called the Greys and about us being propelled into a Fourth Dimension at the turn of the century.

The book claimed that there would be a major pole shift. The ones of us who could manifest a "merkaba," a vibrating energy field like a space ship around our bodies, would be saved and reborn in the Fourth Dimension.

The next day Phillip went to get fabric samples because he wanted to reupholster the bunks before taking off. It would be much cheaper in La Paz, he said. He left Michael and me working on the boat. We worked silently and diligently for a while. Then Michael walked over to me and sat down on the deck.

"What did you think of the book?" he asked. I put down my brush and told him that I wasn't sure, that it was different from anything I had read before.

"It is not an accident that you and I are here in La Paz at this time. There are a lot of us here," he said. "Look around."

I looked at the many white dots of boats that were anchored out as far as one could see. They were like a flock of birds, huddled together. "Why do you think all these boats are here?" he said.

Now that he had mentioned it, it did seem strange. Why had all these boats come to La Paz? There were hundreds of them out there. It was a legitimate question.

"We are here for a reason. We are the ones who are to be enlightened when we move into the next dimension," he said. Then he walked away, and we both started working again, but we continued to talk.

He told me that he had a son named Zorro, or was it Zorin. He told me that he missed him and I heard his voice break. I stopped my brush in midair and I told him that I knew the pain that he was going through because I too had been through a divorce and a custody battle. We discussed other relationships and he asked me if I was lonely. He was as easy to talk to as a woman.

When Phillip came back we were taking a coffee break. He couldn't say anything to us because he had brought a woman out to the boat to help him choose colors and fabrics for the bunks.

The woman was not satisfied with the samples he had and told him to go to another store. He would have to hurry because it was Saturday and all the stores closed at 1 p.m. "As long as you are going ashore, I need to go too. I want to call my lawyer," said Michael.

"I'll go and take my shower now," I said quickly. "I'm done with the rails on the starboard side."

Phillip could hardly refuse these requests because the woman was still there. I grabbed a towel and my shower gear and Michael took an old leather briefcase down from his bunk. We all piled into the shore boat and headed for the marina.

When I was done taking a shower I looked for a cool place to sit down and wait for Phillip and Michael. I found some shade on the cement steps on the far side of the shower building. It was unbearable in the sun. I saw Michael go into the shower and when he came out I called to him.

His hair was wet and standing up on his head. He looked like a kid freshly showered after a basketball game. We sat there and talked and the time flew by.

He told me about his daughter's illness and all they had gone through over it. She was his daughter from a first marriage and had a brain tumor when just a teenager. He started to cry. It brought tears to my eyes. I was thinking about my daughter who had lost a baby and the sadness overwhelmed me. Soon we were weeping together.

It was getting dark now and we both wondered what had happened to Phillip. Did he forget us? Had something happened to him in town? We went to the dingy dock and saw that the shore boat was gone. Fortunately, a couple on the *Rendezvous*, the boat next to Phillip's, were heading back out and would give us a ride.

When we approached the boat, a light shone through the porthole and the skiff was hanging off the stern of the boat. Phillip was aboard, and he was tight-lipped.

"Where were you? I looked all over the marina," he said. Didn't you hear me call?"

We shook our heads, two misbehaving children being chastised, shooting glances at one another. I could sense that Phillip wanted to punish us.

The next day Phillip announced that he needed to send Michael up the mast to fix something. Michael gave me a knowing smile, and got up from the table. He cinched his belt around him. Then he took the belt off, adding a sheath knife to it before he cinched it up again.

I stayed down below puttering because it was another hot day and I didn't want to work on deck. I washed our breakfast cups and bowls in a bucket of water and put the raisins and the granola away. I hung the dish rag on the hook and then I took a paper towel and dried the dishes. Usually we let them drip dry. I cleaned the coffee grinder and smoothed out the bunks. This was my last day here.

Suddenly there was a rattling and thumping and shouts and curses from above. I looked out and saw Michael bound to the mast, his legs and body wrapped tightly around it, high in the air. Phillip had a hold of the halyard and gave one last mighty pull to bring Michael to the top of the mast.

Phillip planned to fasten the halyard to a cleat on deck, but the halyard was being pulled out of his hand. He yelled for help and I scrambled up on deck. The mast, no longer upright, was leaning over in the direction of the bow of the boat.

Another of the stays holding the mast popped loose from the deck and the mast started to fall over farther. The weight of Michael was going to cause the heavy wooden mast to come crashing down on the deck or into the water, and Michael would be pinned underneath it, either being crushed or drowned.

With the mast at about a 45 degree angle, suddenly Michael came flying through the air landing hard on his feet on the deck. I ran to him. His face was white and he rubbed his knee, but otherwise was O.K. He said that he sawed away the rope that bound him to the mast just in time. Otherwise he would have died.

The stays were still swinging like whips around us. Phillip finally caught them. Free of Michael's weight, the mast rested at a peculiar angle until Michael and Phillip could prop it back up again.

The rest of the day the three of us were subdued and worked silently. Michael chose not to go ashore with us to take a shower, he wanted to rest his knee.

When Phillip and I were alone in the shore boat, I brought up the close call that Michael had had. Phillip said, "I knew something like this would happen. He's got bad karma."

I mentioned that it wasn't Michael's fault that the stays gave way. It happened because the fastenings on the deck were weak and rotten. Phillip had no comment.

"You need to replace the stays. Will you have Michael help you?" I asked.

"Absolutely not," said Phillip. "He's got bad energy. The sooner I get him off the boat the better."

At dinner, Michael retold the experience and the feelings he had as he saw the mast start to tilt and he felt it give way—how it took every last ounce of strength that he had in order to saw through the rope with his knife...just in the nick of time. I looked at his boyish, trusting face. I wanted to make love to him that night.

After the meal was finished we exchanged phone numbers. Michael invited me to Pescadero the next time I came to Mexico. Then we all went to bed.

I slipped up into the fo'c'sle, but I left the door to the main salon ajar so I could talk to Michael. Phillip started snoring and I knew he was asleep. I was agitated and lay tossing and turning. The breeze through the open hatch cooled my face, but not my body.

I opened the door a crack wider. The main salon was dark but I knew where Michael was. "Michael, can you come here?" I whispered. I heard him slide out of his upper bunk. I hoped he would not step on Phillip's head who was sleeping below him.

Then he was stealing up into the fo'c'sle. I held my breath.

"Michael, can you lower this hatch cover for me, it's stuck," I said.

Michael quietly hoisted himself onto my bunk and reached over me to loosen the screw. We were two bodies in the bunk together. No words were necessary.

The next day Phillip took both of us ashore. Michael had business with his lawyer and I had a plane to catch. Michael offered to take me to the airport in Phillip's truck, but Phillip would not hear of it. We would drop Michael off at his lawyer's first and then Phillip would take me to the airport.

I went to take a shower while Michael made his phone call. When I came out of the shower, Michael was yelling at some man. He had set his old leather briefcase down on the ground while he was on the phone and the man had run over the briefcase with his jeep, splitting it in two. Michael was terribly upset, even though the man who ran over it offered to replace it.

After we dropped Michael off and were on our way to the airport, I told Phillip what had happened to Michaels's briefcase.

"See, what did I tell you, bad karma," Phillip said.

After I got home I dreamed of Michael for weeks, holding onto the rekindled feelings of love and sex with him for some time. I went to a new age bookstore and bought *Nothing in this Book is True, but It's Exactly How Things Are* to try to keep the memory of Michael alive.

I still have not completely forgotten him. When I take the bus from Los Cabos to La Paz I always look at the side of the road near the town of Pescadero for a ranch with a doughboy swimming pool and a dive shop. There is nothing there.

One time I made a half-hearted attempt to contact Michael. Visiting a friend in Todos Santos, I asked her if she had ever heard of him.

She ground the butt of her cigarette into the ashtray. "Michael Cannon? Stay away from that guy. He's a schizophrenic and a wife-beater. The last time I heard his wife was trying to get him deported."

I cannot believe that Michael was a wife-beater. I prefer to think that the reason I never saw him again was that the aliens had come for him. Or that his beautiful body had been transformed into a merkaba and he was vibrating in the other dimension where he was waiting for me.

A PHOTO JOURNEY

As a kid I had a darkroom in our basement where I developed negatives and made prints of the photos I took. When I worked as a reporter in Eureka I took photos for the paper. I bought a secondhand Voigtländer camera with a damn good lens for $75 in 1959. The following photos were picked out by Hannah and me as the classic ones. The photos were taken between 1962 and 1972 when we cruised back and forth to Mexico and our three children were born. Sometimes I wish I could visit these places and people as they were back then, but in 2019 almost nothing is the same.

"Gerber Baby" on the beach in Santa Barbara

Lovers Beach in 1963

A boy in the little town of Cabo San Lucas

Foreigners came to fish, but Mexicans did the work

It took a strong man to carry a marlin up the beach

During siesta the boys came from school to help

We caught fish dragging a "meat" line as we sailed

Little Huckleberry and Froggy posing by the big marlins

Six brothers in a dugout canoe came to check us out

Huckleberry, sea dog and third mate

Ambassador Sharon communicating in baby talk

Pregnant me and Froggy on Mogote peninsula

Maria Guadalupe de Gidley de Gartland de La Paz (Lupe)
and José Abaroa of the shipyard

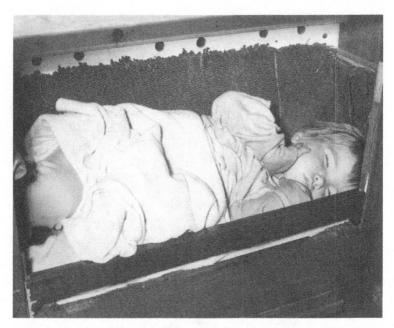

A boat locker was Lupe's bunk on Tia Mia

Big sister Sharon baptizing Lupe with mud

Lupe's bathtub was a bucket

Boys getting around on their burros

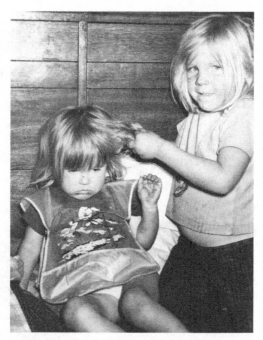

Sharon decided that Lupe needed a haircut

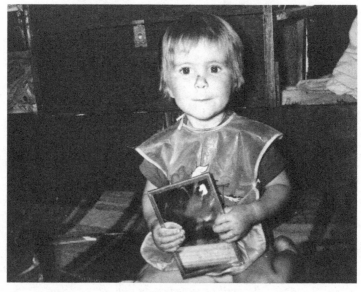

Lupe was happy with her new look

Sharon, age 5, rowing Cass and Lupe ashore

Froggy on her first day of school

Lupe, the flower child

Memo, born 1969, was a messy eater

Lupe climbing the rigging of the Yo Ho Ho

Lupe and Memo, at home on land or sea

273

GOD CREATED CABO SAN LUCAS

When God created Cabo, it was pretty, but very plain.
Just an empty stretch of sand, a sea full of fish, and an unusual formed archway in the sandstone rocks.

The Mexicans who lived there had an outdoor oven bakery, a tiny store, and a little post office in someone's house. A few *machismos* like Ernest Hemingway came to fish. That was O.K. because the fish that were caught were given to the Mexicans who lived on the beach, cleaned the fish, and then divvied it up. The pieces hacked off with a machete fed about the whole town.

Life was going on, but not much "progress" was happening. Years later, God decided (with a little money speaking to him from some *gringos*) that there wasn't enough to do.

So God created some hotels on the sun-struck beach and the tourists came. Each year more came to enjoy the views and the sea and the sand, but God and the *gringos* were still not satisfied.

With the hand of God the tourists multiplied like fishes.

The younger crowd needed more action and so God created the Giggling Marlin where people could hang upside down (women too) and have a lot of fun with tequila pouring down their throats.

When God saw how much fun all his people were having he brought in many servant-slaves from the land to take care of all the tourists and to give them the royal treatment that they deserved.

He built many restaurants and more hotels, some higher than anyone had seen before, then a super highway from the new international airport. He saw to it that cruise ships made the town crawl with fresh blood and money.

The people who owned plastic boats and had the time and money were envious and wanted to come too. So God built marinas and the boats came, two by two, huge white craft with big appetites and engines.

He staffed the beaches with children from the mainland to give the tourists something to buy and something to talk about. Like did you see that little girl selling Chiclets? She was no more than 4 years old.

He brought in parasailing and hang-gliding and jet skis and wave runners and then God rubbed his white hands together and said enough—let's have a party.

Ah, God was so happy. He had accomplished all this in only 30 years. It was his greatest miracle. He could hear the applause rise up to Heaven and he got a big paycheck that year.

But when he looked down from the sky he was puzzled because he couldn't see the beach.

THE END

Made in the USA
Las Vegas, NV
12 October 2023

78979716R00173